Strategic
Planning
for
Fund
Raising

Wesley E. Lindahl

Strategic Planning for Fund Raising

HOW TO BRING IN MORE MONEY USING STRATEGIC RESOURCE ALLOCATION

Jossey-Bass Publishers · San Francisco

For sales outside the United States contact Maxwell Macmillan
International Publishing Group, 866 Third Avenue, New York,
New York 10022.

Manufactured in the United States of America

Library of Congress Cataloging-in-Publication Data

Lindahl, Wesley E., date.
    Strategic planning for fund raising : how to bring in more money
using strategic resource allocation / Wesley E. Lindahl.
        p.   cm. — (The Jossey-Bass nonprofit sector series)
    Includes bibliographical references and index.
    ISBN 1-55542-495-3
    1. Fund raising.   2. Corporations, Nonprofit—Finance.   I. Title.
II. Series.
HG177.L56   1992
658.15'224—dc20   92-25900
                                                              CIP

FIRST EDITION
HB Printing   10 9 8 7 6 5 4 3 2 1   *Code 9296*

The
Jossey-Bass
Nonprofit Sector
Series

To Elom Nelson, my father-in-law, whose enthusiasm for budgeting and planning was contagious and whose courageous struggle with cancer and pneumonia demonstrated what it means to persevere in the face of overwhelming odds.
Peace to his memory.

Contents

Preface

Fund raising in the nonprofit sector has grown tremendously over the past twenty-five years, in terms of both the gift dollars raised and the costs involved in raising those gifts. With so many dollars being spent to raise money, it is of great strategic importance that these dollars be spent in the best way possible. A strategic planning process can assist development officers to achieve this goal.

A strategic planning process for nonprofit fund raising should be based on solid research. However, the growth in fund-raising research has not kept pace with the overall increase in philanthropic support to nonprofits. In addition, most of the research that has been done has involved anecdotal descriptions of how to improve fund raising, based on personal experience and focused on a single fund-raising technique. Also, the confidential nature of fund-raising costs and the difficulty of determining truly comparable fund-raising expenditures from one institution to another have also hampered research efforts, reducing even further the amount of objective research available to assist management in the strategic allocation of fund-raising dollars.

Exceptions do exist, however, where researchers have used techniques typically employed in the social or management sciences to investigate the costs and results of fund raising. The research study that led to *Strategic Planning for Fund Raising* also applied recently established management theory in order to examine fund-raising costs in nonprofit institutions. Instead of comparing costs among similar institutions, the study developed a methodology that each nonprofit organization can configure individually, thereby allowing for the vast differences in nonprofits' potential fund-raising markets.

This book describes a strategic planning methodology for fund raising in nonprofit organizations and illustrates how the methodology was used at Northwestern University, the site of the original study. The methodology allows an institution to optimize gift income by strategically allocating fund-raising resources. Because the methodology can be implemented with varying degrees of complexity, both those institutions that employ only two or three fund-raising programs and those that employ a wide array of programs can apply it.

Audience

The primary audience for this book is management professionals in nonprofit fund-raising operations. This group includes the heads of fund-raising programs and the persons responsible for fund-raising operations within organizations — for example, the director of development for a college within a university or a regional director of fund raising within a national nonprofit organization. A second audience is nonprofit fund-raising support staff who are involved in budget analysis and gift reporting. A third audience is academics who research and teach strategic planning and marketing issues for the nonprofit sector, especially marketing resource allocation issues.

Strategic Planning for Fund Raising can be used by practitioners to help them analyze current fund-raising budgets and develop a strategic allocation plan for future budgets. It can aid the growing group of fund-raising researchers — for example, members of the Association for Research on Nonprofit Organizations and Voluntary Action (ARNOVA) — to understand better the dynamics of the fund-raising process. Finally, the book can be used as a text for a course in strategic planning for nonprofit fund raising.

I assume all readers are familiar with the typical fund-raising programs currently used in nonprofit organizations — for example, direct mail, phone-a-thon, and major gifts. Other more technical topics, such as marginal costs and current valuation of delayed gifts, are introduced at a basic level.

In any book that explains a methodology, especially one that involves organizational planning, there is the potential either to be too much like a cook book and simply offer recipes for procedures or to be too vague about describing process details. I have tried to keep to the middle ground and to provide readers with a description that is organized around typical steps and occurrences, yet is open to the various situations that different fund-raising operations present. The Northwestern University example used throughout is intended only to give a practical illustration of the method as applied in one setting. Each institution is different and should adapt the method for its own use.

Readers of this book may find it useful to read a few additional books about the topic. *Strategic Planning for Public and Nonprofit Organizations,* by J. M. Bryson, considers the overall strategic planning process for nonprofits. *The Costs and Benefits of Deferred Giving,* by N. S. Fink and H. C. Metzler, presents a cost-benefit analysis of the deferred-giving program at Pomona College in California and concludes that deferred-giving programs are very cost effective for universities and colleges. *The Guaranteed Fund-Raising System,* by D. Murray, provides a systems approach to the management of fund raising, but does not provide a way to optimize the fund-raising results through resource allocation.

Overview of the Contents

Chapter One summarizes the strategic planning process in four major phases (mission, strategy, budget, and control) and describes the main benefits of using the methodology. Cautions are given regarding potential internal political challenges to implementing the methodology.

Chapter Two reviews the procedures for setting up the strategic planning process, including selecting the steering committee, which oversees the entire planning process, and scheduling the various planning sessions within the time frame of a fiscal year. Resource allocation categories are introduced and the best way to select appropriate categories is discussed.

An in-depth understanding of past experience is key to successfully predicting a market's reaction to a development effort. When the level of support for a particular program was changed in the past, what was the response? What level of gifts can be anticipated regardless of the level of effort? What is the highest level of gifts possible during an all-out effort? Chapter Three describes how to go about gathering the answers to these questions and converting them into a useable historical analysis. Chapter Three also discusses the Northwestern experience and offers suggestions for nonprofits that lack the resources to compile an in-depth historical analysis.

Historical information alone cannot be used to predict the responsiveness of a market to development effort. Past experience cannot possibly anticipate the future changes in the fund-raising environment. Perhaps the economic climate is changing for the better, or the tax laws have changed, or some internal public relations blunder was made which will affect the level of anticipated giving. Judgmental data from the organization's staff is necessary to help determine how each fund-raising program or market might react to fund-raising effort in the context of a changed environment. Chapter Four describes how to conduct a strategic planning session to capture judgmental data from the development staff. The session includes a Delphi process that involves moving from individual judgments to group discussion and then back to individual judgments until a focused solution is evident. Once again, the Northwestern example is used to illustrate these practices.

Chapter Five defines the relationship between fund-raising effort and gifts received. It describes how to take the data from a historical and judgmental analysis and develop a mathematical model that will predict specific response functions for each program or allocation category.

Once the relationship between costs and gift income is determined for each allocation category, an optimal allocation of costs can be found. Chapter Six presents two approaches for determining the optimal allocation — one involves the use of an electronic spreadsheet and the other, a more complex method, uses outside assistance and special software.

Taking the allocation results from the optimization process and setting a final strategy can be a difficult process. Chapter Seven discusses this process and reviews how to develop a useable strategy.

Chapter Eight describes the control process by which predicted gift levels are checked against actual gift levels to allow for midyear corrections in fund-raising strategy. Especially important to consider is the possibility that outside environmental issues could affect the original mathematical model.

The conclusion summarizes the benefits of the methodology and discusses its implications for all nonprofit institutions. In addition, the Northwestern University example is used to discuss how universities should consider refocusing their basic strategies to move away from short-term programs and favor long-term programs.

Today the demands and pressures on nonprofit organizations to raise more dollars with fewer costs are tremendous. The public is concerned that contributions go directly to the cause and not to pay for fund-raising staff or postage. Nonprofit professionals are aware, however, that it takes money to raise money. But the questions still linger, from the board of directors down to development staff: How much money does it take? And how should that money be used to bring in the most gifts? Using the methodology described in this book, readers can answer these questions specifically for their organization. They can raise more dollars by creating a plan that optimizes gift income through better resource allocation. And they can tell the public, with confidence, that they are using fund-raising dollars as wisely as possible.

Acknowledgments

I wish to express sincere appreciation to my dissertation advisors at Northwestern University—Dean David Wiley, Professor Adris Zoltners, Vice President of Development Ronald Vanden Dorpel, and Professor Christopher Winship—who gave comments and suggestions from diverse perspectives on the original study on which this book is based. Without their support, this project would not have been possible.

The original proposal for the project was developed with the guidance of Professor Norman Bowers during an independent study in the fall of 1987. I also received helpful comments and assistance from Alfred A. Blum, Jr., Mary Crowl, Elom Nelson, Dorothy Speidel, Jonathan Heintzelman, Margaret Lee, Doreen True, Philip Kotler, Scott Meyer, Marie Schneider, William Taylor, Martin Wojcik, and Greg Allebach. Thanks also to all of the staff at Northwestern who faithfully completed each of the questionnaires that came their way. The comments of reviewer Robert Fogal, director of The Fundraising School at Indiana University's Center on Philanthropy, were especially helpful in preparing the final manuscript. The support, encouragement, and guidance of Alan Shrader and the rest of the staff at Jossey-Bass were terrific. Thank you for your unfailing confidence in this project.

Finally, I am indebted to my family—my wife, Deb, and children, Anne and John—for putting up with my long evenings away from home and my sitting in front of the computer while family activities surrounded me. Thanks for the opportunity.

September 1992   Wesley E. Lindahl
                                                             Libertyville, Illinois

The Author

Wesley E. Lindahl is director of development and alumni information services at Northwestern University. He received his B.A. degree (1976), summa cum laude, from North Park College in mathematics; his M.S. degree (1980) from the University of Minnesota, Minneapolis, in mathematics; and his Ph.D. degree (1990) from Northwestern University in administration and policy studies.

Lindahl has spent the last several years studying fund raising in universities and presenting the findings of these studies in various settings. In 1990, he was selected (with Christopher Winship) to prepare "Statistical Models for Prospect Identification," a paper for the Center on Philanthropy Symposium in Indianapolis, Indiana. In 1991, his paper "Differentiating Planned and Major Gift Prospects" won the American Prospect Research Association's Excellence in Writing on Prospect Research Award. He was one of the 1992 recipients of the CASE Grenzebach Award for outstanding dissertations. That dissertation is the basis of this book.

Strategic
Planning
for
Fund
Raising

1

Strategic Planning and Fund Raising: An Overview

According to a study by the American Association of Fund-Raising Counsel (AAFRC Trust for Philanthropy, 1991), philanthropic contributions to nonprofit organizations in the United States grew to $122.5 billion in 1990, up 5.75 percent from 1989. Religious organizations received the largest amount ($65.8 billion), with gifts to education ($12.4 billion), human services ($11.8 billion), and health ($9.9 billion) accounting for most of the balance.

These tremendous amounts are raised by organizations at a cost, especially in the nonreligious categories. In the field of higher education, for example, fund raising, or development costs that involve staff, equipment, and supplies are typically thought to be around 10 percent of the funds raised — or around $1.2 billion in 1990. Development costs for other categories of nonprofits are also likely to be somewhere around this level. In any case, it is safe to say that fund-raising costs account for

1

somewhere between $3 billion and $7 billion spent annually by nonprofits.

Ensuring that these dollars are put to the best use possible should be of prime concern to the organizations spending the funds, the donors supporting the causes, and the fund-raising professionals working to bring in the highest level of support. In a 1991 speech to the Council for Institutional Cooperation, John Hackett, vice president for finance and administration at Indiana University, cautioned the fund-raising community that the demand for cost efficiency by outside interests will become more and more pronounced in the coming years. The public will be insisting that the principles and techniques of corporate management be applied to the management of colleges and universities.

Furthermore, in a recent study, Herman, Weaver, and Heimovics (1991) reported that the percent of the budget used for fund raising was the number one factor in the way respondents judged the effectiveness of a nonprofit organization. Steinberg (1988–1989) discusses the push by government to regulate the fund-raising industry by using the percent fund-raising costs as an indicator of fraud. Although he convincingly argues that this type of indicator may not indicate fraud (it may indicate instead that the nonprofits in question have taken up unpopular causes), still remaining is the public opinion that very low fund-raising costs indicate a well-managed organization.

Therefore, the issue of how best to use the fund-raising dollar should be of strategic concern to most nonprofits and is perhaps the central strategic issue for their development operations. The purpose of this book is to offer a development operation a strategic planning methodology that goes beyond the standard practices of goal setting and gift projections and that provides a means of considering the internal political struggles within the entire organization, the outside constraints and trends, and a wide range of possible action plans. This process allows fund-raising practitioners the opportunity to use their intuition and experience in an organized rigorous way, rather than an ad hoc or anecdotal fashion.

The most fundamental difference between standard fund-raising planning and the strategic planning process described in this book concerns the way individual fund-raising programs are integrated into the planning process. Most development operations currently concentrate on planning each program in relative isolation. For example, the direct-mail schedule, budget, and marketing approaches are usually established independently of the major-gift program. The cost effectiveness of each program is also usually considered separately. If the program is cost effective, it is kept and enhanced over the coming year. If not, it is dropped or scaled back. Comparisons among programs look at costs per dollar raised. Howe (1991, pp. 108–109), for example, reviews the "acceptable" rates for each of six traditional fund-raising areas. Although these rates are helpful as general guidelines, they do not consider the cost-effectiveness relationship between the areas. At Northwestern University, direct-mail costs have been estimated to be around twenty-three cents per dollar raised and phone-a-thon costs around thirty cents per dollar. Does this mean that using direct mail is somehow better than having phone-a-thons? Should additional dollars be allocated to the direct-mail program instead of the phone-a-thon program because the former is more cost effective? Not necessarily. The decision should really depend on the efficiency of the *next* dollar invested in each program.

Suppose, through a careful analysis of past experience and the size and current coverage of the market, that the next $20,000 invested in the phone-a-thon program will return $100,000 in gifts, for a net increase of $80,000 and an efficiency of twenty cents on the dollar. On the other hand, the next $20,000 expended on the direct-mail program is projected to bring in only $40,000 in gifts, for an efficiency of fifty cents per dollar and a net increase of $20,000. In this case, the investment in the phone-a-thon program is projected to be the best of the two investments ($80,000 net increase versus $20,000).

A comparison to the tax system may help to clarify the concept of focusing on the next dollar. Suppose the dividing point between a 28 percent tax rate and a 33 percent tax rate is $50,000. A $49,999 salary is taxed at 28 percent, but the next dollar earned moves the salary into the next tax bracket and that dollar is taxed at 33 percent. Just as the tax rate changes with the salary level, the cost per dollar raised changes with a program's gift level. Just because the rate of return is currently 20 percent does not mean that it will remain at that level.

Clearly, the concept of cost per dollar provides only a static comparison of past efficiency, whereas the concept of the next, or marginal, dollar provides a dynamic comparison among ongoing development programs. The process presented in this book uses this latter concept as the fundamental basis for comparing a nonprofit's fund-raising programs.

Strategic Planning Systems for Fund Raising

Is strategic planning appropriate for all fund-raising operations? Bryson (1988) discusses the usefulness of the strategic planning process to nonprofit organizations and emphasizes that strategic planning is not a single methodology, but rather can be tailored to each particular situation. Bryson describes eight different views of strategic planning, each with advantages and disadvantages for nonprofits. Of these views, the "Strategic Planning Systems" model fits the planning needs of the typical fund-raising office in a nonprofit organization, because it allows management to make, implement, and control important decisions across functions and levels.

Lorange (1980) presents four questions that should be addressed in any strategic planning system:

1.   Mission: Where are we going?
2.   Strategies: How do we get there?
3.   Budgets: What is our blueprint for action?
4.   Control: How do we know if we are on track?

Consider how these four questions might be rephrased for a fund-raising organization.

> *Mission: Where are we going?* Development officers and staff should answer these questions to determine their operation's mission: What are we raising money for? Do we care only about the total dollars we raise? Are we interested in adding to the donor base? Do we wish to increase public awareness of the organization? What

is the time frame for our mission? Can we take five years to wait for a major gift to come in? Do ethics play a role in where we are going? How important is our reputation? How does the mission of the entire organization fit with the mission of the fund-raising operation? These questions, along with others specific to different organizations, should be addressed in the annual planning session.

Strategies: How do we get there? This question requires a review of the fund-raising techniques that might be possible given the prospect base. What are the programs currently in use — direct mail, benefit dinners, auctions, phone-a-thons, major gifts, or planned gifts? How successful have the programs been? How costly have they been? What are other nonprofits doing to raise money? Would those techniques be useful in our organization? In what areas is there the potential for competition? How would incremental changes in the level of development effort for each program affect gift levels in that program and in other programs? After working out the current answers to these questions, development officers can determine a set of potential strategies.

Budgets: What is our blueprint for action? For this question, the methodology calls for an analysis of the various strategies that were proposed above: Given the ways various fund-raising programs are expected to react to increases and decreases in the level of resources allocated, what is the optimal way to allocate these resources? The resulting allocation levels then need to be translated into budget lines and detailed plans of action for each individual program. They will represent the blueprint for the organization's strategic plan for the coming year(s).

Control: How do we know if we are on track? This last question is crucial to the entire process. How often does the development office need to check the projected results against the actual results? Who will check? What criteria will be used? How are pledges and bequest expectancies to be reported? These are questions each operation must deal with individually. One of the mistakes institutions often make in the area of control is to use cash-in gift levels to indicate the performance of their fund-raising operations. This practice can lead to a false sense of how well a program is doing. For programs such as direct mail, cash-in numbers are appropriate. But for estate gifts, multiyear pledge commitments, and irrevocable trusts, cash-in numbers can distort the reporting of fund-raising progress. For example, a large bequest received and reported in the current year but negotiated several years earlier can mask current problems in the planned-giving program.

Asking Lorange's questions in a fund-raising context suggests that the overall structure of a strategic planning systems approach can be appropriate to the nonprofit fund-raising area. Murray (1987) also uses the basic systems approach in his planning model for fund raising because of the way it integrates the various parts of an organization and views the organization as dynamic rather than static.

Stuart (1969) and Galloway (1979) caution us, however, that strategic planning systems taken to the extreme are characterized by substantial comprehensiveness, formal rationality in decision making, and tight control. These extremely rational systems work best in an organization that has a clear mission, clear goals and objectives, centralized authority, clear performance indicators, and extensive information about actual performance available at reasonable cost. Although the strategic planning process described in this book is not at that extreme, it is helpful to consider how well the typical fund-raising operation can measure up to the organizational characteristics that work well with a systems approach.

How clear is the typical fund-raising operation's mission? Certainly the mission will vary among operations, but obviously, the one overriding mission is to meet the resource needs of the nonprofit organization. Therefore, even if a fund-raising staff does not presently have a well-defined mission, by going through a mission-building process, they can usually articulate a clear mission statement.

Are the fund-raising goals or objectives of the typical fund-raising operation clear? Murray (1987, p. 44) divides the objectives of a development office into two parts—monetary objectives, which specify a particular dollar amount as a goal to be raised within the constraints of a preset budget, and non-monetary objectives, which usually relate to levels of participation or solicitation activity. The monetary goals of most operations are certainly clear, although the nonmonetary goals can be unclear at times. Even so, with some creative thought and looking at a few examples, the most common nonmonetary goals can be stated clearly. For example, participation can be quantified as a percentage of those solicited who give a particular gift, and solicitation activity can be stated as the number of personal visits or phone calls made, or direct-mail pieces sent, within a certain time period.

Is there a central authority figure? In no organization is one person ever completely in charge of everything—even if he or she thinks so! Pressures from donors, the board of directors, the public media, the head of the nonprofit, and the fund-raising staff can erode the control of the head of the development department. However, the head of development usually has the power and authority to make many changes, especially in budget allocations and personnel matters. This situation contrasts sharply with the experience most provosts or deans in a university or college face, where collegial governance necessitates a committee approach to most policy issues and personnel decisions. However, some fund-raising operations in particular nonprofits lack any semblance of a central authority figure. In this case, the strategic planning approach may not work.

Are there clear performance indicators in the typical development operation? This question relates back to having clear objectives. Once the objectives are clearly stated, the corresponding performance can usually be determined. The performance indicators needed are usually the dollars raised, the number of new donors, and the number of prospect contact hours or level of other fund-raising activity.

How costly is it for a typical operation to gather performance information? The costs are quite low for two typical indicators, dollar and donor counts, since the receipting process drives the storage of this information. The prospect contact hours are not maintained naturally as a part of a required accounting process and hence could be costly to the nonprofit organization (later, I will discuss how lack of this information may negatively affect the fund-raising operation).

For most development operations, the strategic planning systems model appears to be appropriate and feasible. Exceptions exist, however, and in those situations where the mission is particularly unclear, the objectives are vague, successful performance is difficult to determine, and no central budgeting authority exists, the development officers should reconsider using this approach.

Methodology Overview

The four questions concerning mission, strategies, budgets, and control, although fundamental to the strategic planning concept, need to be placed within the context of a specific methodology that a fund-raising operation can use to actually answer the questions, implement an action blueprint, and achieve the operation's mission. The methodology described in this book is modeled after a process that has been successfully used in the analogous sales or marketing departments of for-profit corporations.

There is a wide body of literature concerning the effective allocations of a sales force by a for-profit corporation. Zoltners and Sinha (1980, p. 244) provide a table of references to work done in this area. In addition, they have developed their own method for determining how a company should allocate its sales resources. Over the past ten years, they have used this approach with hundreds of clients. The method can incorporate multiple time periods, and carryover effects (effort in one year affecting the next year). Although not every feature of the sales force allocation planning process will appear in the fund-raising methodology explained in this book, the concepts, theoretical background, and years of practical experience in sales force allocation situations that underlie the process in the corporate environment also serve to support the process in the fund-raising environment.

Overview of the Strategic
Planning Process for Fund Raising

People sometimes use a paper napkin to quickly sketch ideas. At a breakfast meeting with Philip Kotler in 1987, when I discussed the concepts behind my methodology, I distinctly recall using the paper placemat as a sketch pad in our lively discussion. The overview that follows is an attempt to give the reader a similarly concise picture of each of the nine steps in the strategic planning process for fund-raising operations. In order to illustrate the irreducible basics, I have included an example of the way each step might occur in a very small development office with only two fund-raising programs.

Step One: Identify the Process
Sponsors, Champions, and Analyst

Politics can play a role in deciding whether or not to implement a strategic planning process. Bryson (1988) found that successful strategic planning processes have sponsors who may or may not be active participants, but who make sure others know about the sponsors' desire to see decision makers give the process a good try. These sponsors must be identified. Champions — the committed participants in the process — should also be identified. Champions keep their minds open about the issues that may arise in the process, believe that the process will result in useful answers, and drive hard to see the process to completion. At a minimum, the person in charge of the larger organization and the head development officer need to become involved and committed to the process, because they are the ones who will make the ultimate decision whether to go ahead with it.

Also, unless outside consultants are brought into the process, the services of an internal analyst must be acquired. This person could be anyone in the development office who can work with figures and handle a spreadsheet software package on a PC, has an ability to interact with fund raisers, and is familiar with both the fund-raising budget and the programs.

The champions and the analyst will form a steering committee for the strategic planning process. They should meet at least once every month and more regularly when involved in the specific tasks described in the following steps. It is essential that this committee have as a member the fund-raising operation's lead authority for budgetary allocations — the oversight of this process cannot be delegated exclusively to the analyst or other staff members. A lead authority who is not a member of the steering committee may not trust the results of the process and may leave the blueprint for action gathering dust instead of providing the highest level of fund-raising success.

> In a small development office, this first step may simply consist of the head of the institution and the director of development deciding to begin a strategic planning process based on this book.

Step Two: Determine the Timing of the Planning Sessions

A planning retreat, or series of meetings, will involve the entire development staff (or a representative group if the operation has over twenty fund raisers), along with one or two key staff members from elsewhere in the institution, who will be key players in the entire institution's budgeting process. This retreat must be scheduled to occur at a point early enough to ensure that budgetary decisions will actually affect the budget for the coming fiscal year (or other appropriate period of time — for a capital campaign budget it might be a three-year period), but not so early that the gift dollar totals for the previous year (or other time period) will not be available.

> In the small fund-raising organization, the director schedules a lunch meeting with the heads of the two main fund-raising programs for sometime before budgets for the upcoming year are due but after the current year's gift dollar totals are available.

Step Three: Determine the Allocation Categories

The steering committee for the strategic planning process needs to determine the allocation categories that the process will consider. Usually the fund-raising budget is not set up programmatically, so budget lines can rarely be used as allocation categories. Instead, a matrix approach that considers types of markets, fund-raising techniques, and gift types may be used as a starting point for the discussion. Typical market categories are grateful patients, alumni, other institutional patrons (for example, museum visitors), board members, corporations, foundations, and past donors. Fund-raising techniques usually fall into the categories of direct-mail solicitations, phone-a-thons, personal visits, benefit dinners, auctions, raffles, and volunteer solicitations. Gift types are bequests, outright major gifts, irrevocable trusts (planned gifts), and annual gifts.

In development operations for large nationally based nonprofits or in decentralized university development operations, these categories may be further subdivided by region of the country or by school within the university. These organizations may also want to consider following a separate strategic planning process in each region or other unit, especially if budgetary control does not rest in a single authority.

The categories chosen may need to be changed in the following year's iteration of the process, but all effort should be made to hold categories constant throughout a year in which a strategic plan is being implemented.

> The small organization's development director discusses direct mail and major gifts with the heads of the two main programs. They decide that these two programs are indeed the only ones to consider when allocating development resources.

These first three steps of the strategic planning process are covered in Chapter Two.

Step Four: Perform a Historical Analysis
of Past Giving and Development Effort

In this step, the analyst assembles information from the institution's records regarding past giving levels and fund-raising
effort by category. At the very least, this means going back two
or three years to provide aggregate costs and gift income information from the gift records and budget lines, adjusted to reflect
the allocation categories. If resources are available for a more
extensive investigation, the time period could be lengthened to
ten years.

The historical analysis centers on uncovering the ways
changes in development effort (in terms of effort funding levels)
affect gift income. In a large regional nonprofit, differences between regions using different levels of effort funding could also
be investigated. In most nonprofits, different levels of effort from
year to year will be compared to the results for each of those
years.

After the analyst completes the historical study, the various survey sheets needed for the upcoming strategy sessions can
be designed. One survey sheet is designed for each category,
with the base case (last year's effort and results) clearly indicated to provide a guideline for the survey respondents.

> The heads of the two main programs in the small
> organization prepare for the planning session lunch
> meeting by assembling aggregate costs and benefits
> for each of the two programs over the past five
> years.

The procedures involved in a historical analysis are described in detail in Chapter Three.

Step Five: Hold Strategic Planning
Sessions That Include a Delphi Process

Ideally, the actual strategic planning sessions involving development staff take place at a two-day retreat. However, some de-

velopment offices may have to substitute a series of meetings. The first day's session begins with a discussion of the mission of the fund-raising operation. Is the development office interested in more than the total dollars coming in? Are some categories more important to the nonprofit than others, due to nonfiscal criteria? If some categories are more critical, consensus determines how they should be weighted to reflect their higher value. Next, environmental factors such as tax law changes are discussed to assist the participants in their decision making. If this is the second year of the planning process, a review of past predictions versus current gift income results is then presented to the group and a discussion is held as to the causes of any differences.

Finally, the retreat leader moves the discussion to the issue of how resources allocated to the various fund-raising categories, or programs, could be cut back or increased in the coming year. Once a scenario is developed that shows how increases or decreases in each category's funding level might be specified, the participants are asked to predict gift income based on those various funding levels. This is the beginning of the Delphi process. The surveys are completed individually, but are later assembled by the analyst into a single graphical representation for each category.

In the second day's session, the respondents are asked to discuss the results from the first day and to defend their outlying responses. A second set of survey sheets is then handed out and responses are gathered individually. The results are sent around to participants in the following weeks.

> At their lunch meeting, the director of development and the two program heads agree that the mission of the development office is to raise money, with special emphasis on current-year dollars. They also agree that direct mail dollars are "worth" 1.5 times major-gift dollars because they more closely reflect the mission. After spending a few minutes telling about past costs and results for the two programs, the three officers come up with three different pos-

sible funding levels for each of the two programs —
less than last year's, equal to last year's, and more
than last year's. They could fund direct mail at a
$40,000, $60,000, or $100,000 level. They set pos-
sible funding levels for major gifts at $100,000,
$130,000, and $150,000.

      The three fund raisers write down their pre-
dictions of how many dollars might come in at each
of the three funding levels. The three then reveal
their answers and discuss the reasons for their
choices. Then they individually predict again.

This step of the process is discussed in Chapter Four.

Step Six: Build Models for the Allocation Categories

Based on the information from the second set of surveys, the
analyst determines the average predicted gift values for each level
of funding within each category. This can be done in several ways,
from simply visually locating the "middle" response value for each
effort level on a graph, to running a statistical program to determine a formula that will work for the selected levels and for any
intermediate resource level as well. Using either approach, a set
of potential strategies will be produced that consists of various
combinations of funding levels for the different categories.

      The three officers eliminate the high and the low
for each category from their second round of predictions. They are left with the projections shown in
Table 1.1. Direct-mail gifts have been multiplied
by 1.5 in accordance with the officers' earlier decision that direct-mail dollars are more valuable to
the institution than major-gift dollars.

      Chapter Five presents a comprehensive approach to model
building.

Step Seven: Determine the Optimal Strategy

Given the set of potential strategies, which one will serve to optimize the adjusted net gift income over the coming year? The

Table 1.1. Simple Model for Predicting Gift Income.
(In thousands of dollars)

Program	Costs	Gifts Projected	Adjustment Factor	Gifts Adjusted
Direct mail	40	210	× 1.5	315
	60	240	× 1.5	360
	100	300	× 1.5	450
Major gifts	100	700		700
	130	800		800
	150	860		860

analyst examines the strategies using a computer program and determines the optimal strategy. In more complicated cases, when an outside consultant is hired in the process, specialized software routines are used to determine the correct optimization point.

To determine their optimal strategy, the three development officers check each of the possible funding combinations for the amount of gifts that would be generated (Table 1.2). The optimal resource allocation appears in the last line shown on the table, where $100,000 is set for the direct-mail program and $150,000 for the major-gift program. If the total dollars must equal last year's budget ($60,000 + $130,000 = $190,000), then the optimal allocation

Table 1.2. Simple Model for Optimizing Gift Income.
(In thousands of dollars)

Direct-Mail Costs	Major-Gift Costs	Total Costs	Total Net Gifts
40	100	140	(315 + 700 − 140) = 875
40	130	170	(315 + 800 − 170) = 945
40	150	190	(315 + 860 − 190) = 985
60	100	160	(360 + 700 − 160) = 900
60	130	190	(360 + 800 − 190) = 970
60	150	210	(360 + 860 − 210) = 1,010
100	100	200	(450 + 700 − 200) = 950
100	130	230	(450 + 800 − 230) = 1,020
100	150	250	(450 + 860 − 250) = 1,060

is shown on line three, where the cost of the direct-mail effort is reduced by $20,000 from last year's level and major-gift effort is increased by $20,000.

Two approaches for determining an optimal allocation strategy are discussed in Chapter Six.

Step Eight: Convert Optimal Strategy into a Budget Blueprint

The steering committee meets to review the results of the optimization analysis and to set the actual strategy. A raw result from the computer is translated into a workable budget plan, or blueprint for action, for the coming year. This is done in collaboration with the regular budget committee, if there is one.

> The three officers from the small development office note that the optimal allocation level is difficult to build into the budget because the direct-mail staff is not up to speed in major-gift fund raising. The three finally agree to spend $5,000 in training over year one, and then, in year two, to increase the major-gift funding level by $35,000. This represents a funding investment of $20,000 per year over two years.

Chapter Seven presents a steering committee's options for setting a practical budget.

Step Nine: Arrange for Feedback and Control

Meetings should be scheduled periodically for the development staff to review results to date and to make recommendations for midterm corrections—especially in cases where environmental factors have changed. The strategic planning retreat for the next year will provide a further opportunity to review the results.

> Every couple of months, the three development officers schedule a lunch meeting to review how the

actual results differ from the predicted results. Mid-year corrections are made. At the end of the year, new allocations are developed, and the process continues.

The techniques for ensuring good feedback and control are presented in Chapter Eight.

The Northwestern University Example

The analysis done at Northwestern University will be used as an example throughout the book, and the results summarized in Chapter Nine. Since the university setting involves complications that might not exist at other nonprofits, I will also present examples of each of the basic ideas that will be applicable to any type and size of nonprofit.

For readers unfamiliar with Northwestern University, the following description may be helpful. Northwestern University is a major, private, research-oriented institution of higher education. Twelve schools make up the university, including professional schools of law, medicine, business, and dentistry. The medical centers associated with the university are all independent, and their gifts are reported independently.

The Office of University Development and Alumni Relations has several subdivisions. Alumni Relations sponsors programs and activities for alumni, such as reunions and regional alumni club events. Annual Giving is responsible for the direct-mail and phone-a-thon programs for the undergraduate schools. Planned and Major Gifts (the result of a recent merger between the estate-planning group and the major-gift group) provides a regionally based program for estate-planning and major-gift fund raising. The professional schools each have a fund-raising staff, as well as alumni program staff. True single purpose capital campaigns are set up through the associated schools but coordinated centrally in the vice president's office. Development and Alumni Information Services maintains the data base of almost 300,000 records and provides research services to the major-gift staff.

Northwestern's fund-raising program is distinguished in several ways. The estate-planning program is well established, raising between $2 million and $9 million per year in irrevocable trusts during the six years analyzed in the study (fiscal years 1982–83 through 1987–88). Another distinguishing element is the fact that the alumni donor base was increased dramatically in the late seventies and early eighties. The annual-fund phone-a-thon and direct-mail programs were increased during the years directly before the study began. Finally, the parents' program is not extensive at Northwestern. Over the years of the study only approximately one full-time equivalent (FTE) staff member was assigned to the parents' program.

Northwestern's fund-raising program has grown over the past fifteen years. In the early 1980s, the direct line development staff numbered less than twenty-five. By 1986, the staff had grown to around forty, but is currently in the midthirties. Gift levels grew from the twenty millions to the seventy millions over this time period.

Northwestern has not had much experience using the strategic planning process, compared to corporations that have been using these techniques for years. However, the experience it has had to date shows that the process, which was developed in the for-profit community, can be implemented in fund-raising nonprofits. The results from the first round in the process, described in Chapter Eight, show that those of us on the development staff were a bit optimistic in our projections. However, many of the changes that were made to the allocation levels may not show up in the gift numbers for a couple of years, and furthermore, no one correctly predicted the effect on giving of the national recession in 1990–91 — especially in the corporate market.

No strategic planning process, whether based on analysis or intuition, can predict with certainty the outcomes of a particular strategy. What is important is whether the process can provide a forum to integrate the available information about the organization and its environment into a meaningful strategic plan of action.

Benefits and Challenges of Strategic Planning

What are the benefits to a development office that uses the strategic planning process I have outlined? First, within the limits of the assumptions that go into the process, strategic planning will enable the nonprofit to spend its fund-raising resources in the most efficient way possible. Second, management will be better able to determine the performance of fund-raising staff. Goals will be more realistic, because they will relate to the level of resources allocated. Third, because of staff participation in developing the plan, staff members will be more committed to the final plan. Fourth, the development office will learn more about the ways its fund-raising markets and programs actually function. Fifth, the key decision makers will be discussing the most important issues of the whole fund-raising operation — not just each decision maker's small area of interest. The decision makers will be able to move from a short- to a long-term horizon and to ensure that the mission of the organization is considered in the process.

Finally, a word of caution is in order for those about to implement strategic planning. Bryson (1988) mentions several challenges that can slow down or stall any attempt to set up a planning process. First, there is the "human problem" of getting the attention and support of management in the process (p. 200). At least one sponsor and one champion are crucial to the process. Second, there is the "process problem" of trying to sell the ideas to staff and others (p. 208). Third, there is the "structural problem" of trying to get each of the parts of an operation to act like the whole (p. 211). The question of how to involve the implementers in the planning process is also a part of this third challenge. And the fourth challenge is the "institutional problem" of the lack of strong leadership — a challenge many organizations face (p. 213).

The task of planning will not be easy, but the process can be well worth the effort. The potential for increased gift resources for nonprofits is great and is worth the risk of spending time structuring a process that organizes the intuition and experience of fund raisers into meaningful strategic plans of action. Furthermore, because there are several different levels at which the process can be implemented, a fund-raising operation can start slowly and work through the years to fully implement the process. In a twist on a well-known cliché: Anything that is really worth doing is worth doing modestly, at first!

2

Setting Up
the Strategic Planning
Process

Politics plays a big role in the strategic planning process, especially in the early preplanning stages when the support of key
decision makers is sought. The approach to getting that support depends heavily on where the person seeking the support
is in the process. The director of a nonprofit organization's entire fund-raising operation who also controls the allocation of
resources to the various fund-raising programs needs to focus
on getting the support of the head of the entire organization
and of the board of directors at the management level.

Typically, management is receptive to strategic planning
but may be concerned that the costs will be too high. Most of
the costs, however, are staff costs, although financial expenditures may be involved if a consultant is brought in. In any case,
a proposal should be prepared and presented that outlines the
projected costs and results of the strategic planning process. After
the head of the organization and the board of directors sign on
to the process, the fund-raising staff must be brought "on board"

as well. The cooperation of the development staff will probably be less difficult to obtain.

A staff member, such as a development officer who was involved in several different fund-raising programs over the years and is currently in charge of a program, may think there is a need to examine the mission of the fund-raising operation, to consider different strategies of resource allocation in a more structured way than is currently done, to agree on an optimal departmentwide strategy, and to implement the plan with feedback provided on a regular basis to all staff members. If so, this officer must convince the director of development, and perhaps the head of the entire organization, to proceed with a strategic planning process. One way to do this is to first gain the support of the person who could play the role of the analyst in the strategic planning process. Perhaps the person who currently prepares the progress report from the donor data base could be asked to review a section of this book. Together, the officer and the analyst might prepare a presentation to the director of development and the head of the nonprofit in order to convince them of the benefits of the process.

Finally, the person who prepares the monthly development progress reports may be interested in a planning process that will provide a more accurate accounting of development progress. Every bequest received and counted in the current year's results creates a false impression of the department's current-year success. In other, less dramatic, cases, smaller differences in the timing between a solicitation and the eventual receipt of the gift still add up to inaccurate progress statements. If resources are allocated based on these biased reports, they will not be allocated correctly. The analyst sees that properly allocated resources might bring in thousands of extra dollars for little additional cost. Of the three scenarios — interest emanating from management, staff, or analyst — the analyst's situation is the most difficult. The analyst must convince the development staff, the director of development, and the head of the organization to participate in the planning process. Perhaps first convincing a key development officer is an appropriate approach. Then the idea can be presented as a joint proposal to the director and the head. However, if management is not totally dedicated to the process after the presentation has been made, the process should not be attempted.

In larger organizations that consist of regional and central units, the politics involved can be even more pervasive. Bryson (1988) suggests that limits need to be placed on the process in order to achieve an agreement among key decision makers. Perhaps certain minimal resource levels will be off the table in the strategic process so that, for example, each regional unit (or school within a university) will retain a level of funding within 10 percent of last year's budget. In some cases, a large diversified organization may need to set up a separate strategic planning process for each unit, especially if the units are funded locally.

Convincing others to participate in the strategic planning process may be easier if the following points are clearly articulated. The points can be a part of any proposal or presentation but should be tailored to the particular needs of the organization.

- An enormous amount of money is spent on this organization's fund-raising programs, and this process will help us ensure that the dollars are spent wisely.
- For-profit organizations have successfully used this process in the analogous sales force allocation planning process for many years.
- Most out-of-pocket expenses will be minimal; most of the cost is in terms of management staff time. What better use of management time is there than for planning?
- Staff morale should increase because goals and reported results will be more meaningful and motivating. For example, timely reports will reflect ongoing results from the current year's solicitation efforts. Management will be able to monitor staff performance more easily and accurately.
- Communication will increase among staff from different programs. Staff will see themselves as part of the strategy for achieving the mission of the entire organization.
- The staff from all development areas will have a better understanding of the various markets and programs through this process.

- The key decision makers will be discussing the most important issues of the whole fund-raising operation — not just their small areas of interest.
- The focus in planning will move from a short- to a long-term horizon.

The Functions of the Steering Committee

Once the key players in the process reach an agreement (either formal or informal), they will form a strategic planning steering committee to set up the timing of the planning sessions, select members of the Delphi planning group, and determine the allocation categories that will be a key part of the framework of the process. A three-person committee is recommended, although in a large operation the size may need to be increased. The three that must be involved are the director of development (who controls the fund-raising budget) as either a champion or sponsor, the director of development services (who controls the data base and produces reports) as the analyst, and either a strong development officer as a champion or (for small organizations) the head of the entire organization as a sponsor. It is worth repeating that it is essential that this committee have as a member the lead authority for budgetary allocation in the fund-raising operation — the oversight of the planning process cannot be delegated exclusively to any other staff member. A lead authority who is not involved in working out a strategic plan is likely to distrust that plan and fail to follow through on it.

Once the steering committee is set up, the sponsors, the champions, and the analyst on this committee should meet at least once every month, and more regularly when involved in initial planning, determining categories, and preparing for Delphi sessions at a retreat or other meeting setting.

At their first meeting, they will set up the schedule for the planning session that may involve all development staff in a small organization and up to twenty key staff members in a large organization. In order to apply strategic planning in setting the budget for the coming year, the timing of the major planning session is very important. As discussed in the last chapter, a time must be chosen that is just before the budget process occurs and just after the yearend reports are ready for distribution. Suppose the fiscal year ends June 30, and the final budget for the fiscal year must be set by March 30, three months earlier. A late fall retreat would fit the criteria since the June final results for the previous year would be available and the decisions from the retreat could be a part of the following year's fiscal budget. For nonprofits whose fiscal year ends in December, a retreat in the spring of the following year would allow results to be available for planning the budget for the year after.

Besides this retreat, periodic meetings should be set to compare progress to date to predictions, to renew participants' commitment to the planning process, and to allow for midcourse corrections — especially those necessitated by external changes such as the onset of a recession or revisions in the tax law. During the second year of the process, the retreat will also provide an opportunity to examine progress to date and to use the results of that analysis to change the current budget as well as the coming year's budget.

The steering committee then needs to consider other details in the process. Will a consultant be used or will all of the analysis and facilitation be handled internally? What other subcommittees might be needed? What is the scope of the planning process? Which departments should be involved? What is the representation needed for the Delphi process? Should a full presentation explaining the process be made to staff? When should it take place? Who will handle the arrangements and create presentation materials? Because of the differences in size among nonprofit development operations, some of these questions will not need to be addressed. The steering committee needs to consider only the most pertinent procedural issues.

Identification of Allocation Categories

One of the most important tasks of the steering committee is to identify allocation categories. These categories should stay relatively fixed throughout the strategic planning process, so considerable thought needs to be assigned to this determination.

Each nonprofit has a set of fund-raising programs it has used over the years. This set provides an excellent starting point for discussion; however, the steering committee should not forget to consider whether there are opportunities to try new programs and markets as well.

An example of the categories that might be used in a very simple case would include a phone-a-thon program, a direct-mail program, and programs that seek major gifts from individuals, major gifts from foundations, and major gifts from corporations. Most organizations can determine the resources and the resulting gifts for each of these categories, or programs. These categories are also understandable across institutions — most fund raisers are familiar with the categories and the activities associated with them.

In terms of organizational structure, categories such as these typically consist of people organized into subdepartments, each of which shares a common fund-raising technique or market. However, any distinctly fundable fund-raising activity (and the staff behind that activity) can be considered a resource allocation unit. There are also traditional categories for many nonprofits. For example, the traditional categories for educational institutions are articulated in the Council for Aid to Education (CFAE) report, which has been published for many years for the higher education community.

The CFAE report features fiscally based gift income totals and subtotals by category as a means of comparing and ranking institutions. Typically, gifts are categorized by "sources" — alumni, parents, nonalumni friends, foundations, corporations, religious organizations, fund-raising consortia, and other nonindividuals. Each of these groups is often segmented further into the categories of annual-fund gift (operating funds for current-year expenses), major outright gifts (capital funds for endowments and buildings), irrevocable trusts (legal instruments under which a nonprofit pays the interest on a trust fund to the donor until the donor's death), and bequests (revocable arrangements made in a donor's will or insurance policy).

Traditional development techniques, or solicitation methods, are representations by personal development staff or volunteers, direct-mail programs, benefits/fund raisers, and phone-a-thon programs. A personal visitation program usually includes several stages of cultivation — invitation to lunches, dinners, and school sporting events; phone calls; school/area contacts by deans, coaches and faculty; involvement in academic or program planning through such vehicles as advisory committees; and finally personal solicitation. A direct-mail program involves sending informational material concerning a particular fund-raising area along with a solicitation card and return envelope on a regular basis to donors, activity participants, volunteers, alumni, board members, parents, patrons, and friends. A benefit/fund raiser is a dinner, event, or program that is often underwritten by an individual or organization and that requires the participants to contribute a certain amount over the cost of the dinner or program, or to sign up for contributions for some accomplishment such as every hour danced or mile walked by volunteers at the event. A phone-a-thon program provides annual direct phone contact either by paid staff or by volunteers such as alumni, students, donors, or patrons.

What allocation categories, then, are most reasonable, given the rather broad concept of a category as being any distinctly fundable fund-raising activity? Should the categories reflect traditional breakout categories, such as those on the CFAE report? Or should each development officer become a category? Or should the various programs that may have developed over the years at a particular institution be considered the categories? Or should the categories correspond to the budget lines that have guided management in the past? These are the questions the strategic planning process should answer for each operation.

As an aid in category determination, four general principles should be considered, even though no categorization plan will perfectly follow all of them. First, each category should be well defined. In other words, the definitions of the funds expended and the gifts raised by the unit must be as clear and precise as possible. For example, if each development officer is considered to be a category, the resources associated with that category could be unambiguously defined by the development officer's salary, fringe benefits, and clerical support costs. However, the resulting gifts, because they could involve actions from more than one category, or officer, over several years (through personal cultivation and phone-a-thon and direct-mail programs) are not as definable.

Second, the resources allocated and the corresponding funds generated by the well-defined category should be traceable in the accounting system. This can be a problem regardless of the way a particular category is defined. Even in the simple case of a traditional phone-a-thon program in which the donor response cards are tagged, there is no guarantee that every single donor will insert the correct card with the gift. This is especially true in the case of a strong direct-mail program that sends out solicitations throughout the year. In this instance, designating the entire direct-mail program — rather than each mass mailing — as a category might be more accurate. Even more problematic is the case when the resource allocation categories are traditional budget lines. Except when certain lines (such as phone-a-thon budget lines) taken as a group represent a particular category, the resulting gifts are typically never tagged back to the resources expended to get them.

Third, the categories should be commonly applicable from institution to institution and not unique to a particular organization. Comparisons from one institution to another help in setting realistic goals during the planning process. However, any significant deviation from the current internal organizational structure also brings about the need to consider the cost of the reorganization itself. Maintaining a somewhat traditional structure builds in a level of efficiency. In other words, if the various programs that were developed at a particular institution over the years are used as categories, they may not have a counterpart at other nonprofits. On the other hand, reorganization that involves funding reallocations for the various programs based on a new budgeting pattern may carry with it costs that are indeed present, but difficult to determine. Therefore, the categories need to be set up with as much commonality as possible, but within the bounds of the anticipated cost of changing the current internal divisional structure.

Fourth, categories should be selected so that there is a difference between the ways they react to development efforts.

If additional funding to category A brings in the exact same gift level as additional funding to category B, it will not matter which is funded. Either will produce the same results. If there are few differences between the categories' responses to resources allocated, the allocation of resources among categories is less meaningful. The process of ensuring the greatest differences among categories is referred to as maximizing the distinctiveness in the functional relationship between the resources allocated and the gift revenue generated.

For example, in universities, if the standard budget lines that divide costs by schools are used as categories, there may be two schools that have basically the same relationship between the costs of fund raising and the resulting gifts. How do development officers decide which school will benefit the most from more resources? As far as cost effectiveness is concerned, it does not matter which school gets the additional resources. The responsiveness to fund-raising dollars would be the same.

Maximizing this distinctiveness without formally conducting several studies with different category structures is quite difficult. However, in practice, staff intuition can serve to guide the category selection process. Understanding the concept of maximum distinctiveness and using it as a goal for category determination helps to provide more appropriate category choices.

How would the earlier, simple example of five categories (phone-a-thon, direct mail, and major gifts from individuals, foundations, and corporations) stand up to the four principles I have outlined? For most organizations, this categorization would probably pass muster. Each of the five categories is usually well-defined in terms of both its costs and its gifts. In most organizations, the costs and gifts associated with these categories are traceable in the accounting system. The five categories are usually understood from institution to institution. And finally, intuition suggests that each of the categories (perhaps with the exception of major gifts from corporations and from foundations) would have a distinctive relationship between resources and results. Moreover, the similarity between the categories involving major gifts from corporations and foundations can be handled by combining them into one "nonindividual" category.

Once the categories are determined, the analyst will need to make sure that both the effort levels and gift income amounts for the categories can be determined historically over at least two or three years. Also, it is important to be able to relate categories back to the budget when the time comes for translating the strategy into a blueprint for action.

The following section discusses how allocation categories were set up at Northwestern University. In other nonprofits, there may be fewer categories. Since the cost of the strategic planning process increases with the complexity of the category structure, having fewer categories may be advantageous. It may be worthwhile to start simply and then increase the complexity with each yearly iteration of the process.

Northwestern University Allocation Categories

At Northwestern University, of all the candidates considered as possible categories, a modified traditional category structure, stemming from the CFAE report, came closest to meeting all four category selection criteria. Each category was defined by three elements: markets, techniques, and types of gifts. To begin with, this category structure differentiated six markets: alumni, parents, nonalumni, corporations, foundations, and other nonindividuals (fund-raising consortia and religious organizations were combined in the latter category).

Since these are traditional, well-defined markets, reporting gift results was entirely straightforward. Monitoring the allocation of resources to these markets was slightly more difficult because one development officer could be splitting time among several markets. However, even when this was the case, most officers were aware of the markets they were working with as being distinct entities—perhaps with the exception of parents as opposed to nonalumni. When asked via questionnaire, officers were able to reconstruct the division of their labor among markets without much difficulty.

Finally, looking at aggregate figures, the markets appeared to possess reasonably distinct response functions. For example, the raw figures for 1987–88 indicated the extreme differences among market categories on the basis of average gift size, cost

Table 2.1. Northwestern University 1987–88
Cost per Gift by Market.
(In dollars)

Market	Average Gift	Cost per $1.00	Cost per Transaction
Alumni	690	.067	46
Parents	880	.173	151
Nonalumni	3,100	.022	69
Corporate	3,880	.021	83
Foundations	17,960	.025	453
Other nonindividuals	5,360	(no cost)	(no cost)

per $1.00 raised, and cost per gift transaction (Table 2.1). (De-finitions of costs are described in detail in Chapter Three — included here are direct development staff, secretarial, telephone, postal, and travel costs.)

Each market was subdivided by technique. The three most common techniques in university fund raising are direct mail, phone-a-thon, and personal/other, which covers personal calls and visits and any techniques not a part of direct-mail, phone-a-thon, or personal solicitation programs. Typically, record keeping provides precise differentiation among these techniques, both for resources allocated and gifts received. Using the North-western figures from 1987–88, it also appeared that these categories of techniques possessed distinct response functions (Table 2.2).

Subdividing markets and techniques further, a distinc-tion was made among types of gifts. The CFAE report subdivides

Table 2.2. Northwestern University 1987–88
Cost per Gift by Technique.
(In dollars)

Technique	Average Gift	Cost per $1.00	Cost per Transaction
Personal/other	4,130	.029	118
Phone-a-thon	60	.297	19
Direct mail	130	.231	30

the main matrix into operating and capital funds. Further subdivision, in a separate area of the report, distinguishes between irrevocable trust arrangements and bequests. Combining these four groups and adjusting definitions slightly resulted in the following types of gifts: major outright (an outright or pledged gift equal to or over $5,000 in operating funds, or equal to or over $1,000 in capital funds); annual (an outright or pledged gift under $5,000 in operating funds, or under $1,000 in capital funds); irrevocable trusts; and bequests.

Although slightly modified from the CFAE report, the definitions could be used generally from institution to institution. Reporting results in these categories is usually simple, based on how the gifts are coded in the computer system. The allocation of resources to the raising of certain types of gifts is not as clear cut. Occasionally, an officer is not aware of the type of gift sought until a meeting with the prospect occurs. But in most cases, such as phone-a-thon and direct-mail programs, the development officer is consciously working for a particular type of gift. Even in personal solicitation of individuals, a primary objective is usually determined before the visit.

Once again, the Northwestern example provides a dramatic indication of just how different these gift types can be (Table 2.3).

Combining the markets, techniques, and types into a matrix provided a list of all the possible categories that could be considered at Northwestern University. These categories allowed comparison from institution to institution, and provided distinct reporting groups for resources allocated and funds re-

Table 2.3. Northwestern University 1987–88
Cost per Gift by Gift Type.
(In dollars)

Gift Type	Average Gift	Cost per $1.00	Cost per Transaction
Major outright	22,690	.032	687
Annual	163	.143	23
Irrevocable	196,540	.017	3,239
Bequest	68,620	.018	1,250

ceived. From the raw cost and income numbers from North-western's 1987–88 results (Tables 2.1, 2.2, and 2.3), it seemed likely that there was enough difference in response functions among categories to provide a meaningful variation in the dollars raised when costs were reallocated from one category to another.

Table 2.4 shows the matrix of techniques, gift types, and markets used at Northwestern University. The matrix results in seventy-two possible categories, not all of which will be used by any one development operation. Each category actually used at Northwestern is referred to by a three letter acronym. The first letter represents the market, the second the technique, and the third the gift type. For example, APA is the alumni-personal-annual program, PDA is the parents–direct-mail–annual program, and so forth.

Table 2.4. Northwestern University 1987–1988 Matrix of Categories.

Technique and Gift Type	Market					
	Alumni (A)	Parents (P)	Nonalumni (N)	Corporate (C)	Foundations (F)	Other (O)
Personal/other (P)						
(includes no formal solicitation)						
Annual (A)	APA	PPA	NPA	CPA	FPA	—
Major (M)	APM	PPM	NPM	CPM	FPM	—
Irrevocable (I)	API	—	NPI	—	—	—
Bequest (B)	APB	—	NPB	—	—	—
Phone-a-thon (H)						
Annual (A)	AHA	—	—	—	—	—
Major (M)	—	—	—	—	—	—
Irrevocable (I)	—	—	—	—	—	—
Bequest (B)	—	—	—	—	—	—
Direct mail (D)						
Annual (A)	ADA	PDA	—	—	—	—
Major (M)	—	—	—	—	—	—
Irrevocable (I)	—	—	—	—	—	—
Bequest (B)	—	—	—	—	—	—

3

Gathering
and Analyzing
Historical Data

A historical analysis of an institution's fund-raising operation can range from a simple accounting of aggregate costs and gifts over the prior three years to a full-blown year-long project involving analysis at the detail level for each category going back ten to fifteen years. Most organizations should start simply and work gradually toward a more complex historical analysis. It is much better to have only rudimentary historical information and an active planning process than to focus on historical analysis to the point of stopping the strategic planning process. The fact that the total strategic planning process combines both past experiences and the judgmental insight of development staff members allows for some latitude in the collection of historical data.

This chapter is designed to parallel the way an organization may approach historical analysis. The structure is from simple to complex. The end of the chapter mentions some of the ways Northwestern University data was analyzed. Not all of these approaches proved fruitful in the final strategic planning process. However, all of the approaches are guaranteed to stimulate further thought and discussion by those who value investigating the inside story of the asking-giving process. (Readers interested in the technical aspects of a historical analysis will find a fuller description in Lindahl, 1990.)

How Far to Trust History

When a historical analysis is completed at the appropriate level of complexity, can development staff really use it as a guide to predict future responses of a particular market or program to a development effort? Certainly in some programs the results will be more useful than in others. For example, direct-mail programs will provide statistically more accurate results than bequest programs, simply because of the greater number of solicitations and gifts.

Also, the fact that a very small number of gifts account for the great majority of gift dollars creates problems in every category. A recent gift of ten million dollars from an individual to Northwestern University represents more dollars than were given by all twenty thousand–plus direct-mail donors combined. A rare phone-a-thon gift of one hundred thousand dollars given several years ago accounted for around one-fifth of all dollars given through the phone-a-thon program that year. Therefore, the concept of an "average gift" is difficult to pin down.

Furthermore, a historical analysis of some categories may be suspect because of a long time delay between a solicitation and the final gift. There may also be extenuating circumstances, such as tax law changes or the start up of a new program, that should be considered before using the analysis directly to predict the future. No historical analysis is going to be perfect. That is why the remainder of the strategic planning process is designed to balance the organization's past experiences with the development staff's common sense and in-depth understanding of the current conditions of their external markets and internal fund-raising programs.

Objectives of the Analysis

Before beginning the historical analysis, the analyst should review the objectives of the study with the rest of the steering committee. This will prevent the potential problem of spending time and money to find answers to questions that are not pertinent to the particular institution's planning process. There are also certain questions that must be answered in order to present the results in a format easily used in the Delphi process. Other questions may produce answers that are helpful to the planning participants in understanding the fund-raising process.

At a minimum, the historical analysis needs to provide total costs and gifts for each category for the past three to six years, an estimate of the level of gift income that would come in through each category with very little or no development effort, or funding, and an estimate of the level of gift income that would come in through each category with an all-out development effort. The analysis should also identify categories where the effort in one category produces results in another (crossover) and categories where the past year's efforts affect the current year's results (carryover).

The main objective of the analysis is to provide samples of variation between development efforts in dollars expended and results in gifts received, so as to flesh out the hypothetical cost-gift income curve for each category. If the resources allocated to the effort in one category went from \$100,000 to \$200,000 over two years, what was the response on the gifts side? If one regional office spent \$1,500,000 in fund-raising costs and another regional office spent \$500,000, what was the difference in response? The more data points there are that show costs and results, the more the curve is fleshed out.

Paton (1986, p. 24) and Steinberg (1985, p. 11) describe the theory behind the structure of this curve. At the low end, very little effort will still bring in a certain level of "over-the-transom" gifts. Despite the saying that people give only if asked, a few donors actually send in checks completely on their own. However, the gifts begin coming in at a much stronger pace only when a program gets funded at some reasonable "critical mass" level. Finally, when the market is saturated, additional effort produces only minor increases in gifts. Eventually, the additional benefits will not equal the added expenses.

Figure 3.1, which was taken from the alumni–direct-mail–annual program at Northwestern University, shows the form of the curve used in the strategic planning process described in this book. The horizontal axis represents the development effort level in thousands of dollars, while the vertical axis represents the gifts raised in millions of dollars. As the fund-raising effort increases from $0 to $500,000, the projected level of direct-mail income moves from just over $0 to $2,500,000. Allocating another $500,000 to the effort only increases gifts to $3,500,000. At an effort costing $1,500,000, the curve levels off. There is little projected gain beyond this level. (The mathematical structure of the curve is described in Chapter Five.)

Determining the specific form of the cost-gift curve can be done in two main ways: by looking for changes in effort

**Figure 3.1. Northwestern University
Alumni–Direct-Mail–Annual
Development Effort Response Curve.**

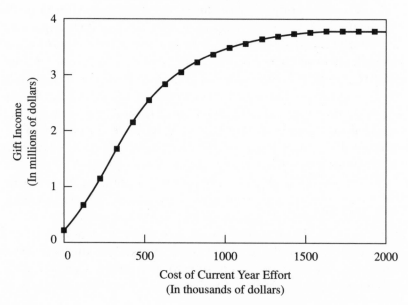

levels from year to year or, in multiregion offices, by looking for changes in effort levels from region to region (assuming similar prospect pools). Suppose a development officer looks for changes in effort levels and results from year to year in a direct-mail program. The initial result of that analysis can be summarized in a table (see Table 3.1). A table for regional comparisons would break out the information by regions instead of years. These data points (costs by gift income) are graphed onto a curve. This curve then provides a projection for each possible funding level. The more data points, the better the "true" underlying curve is revealed. Figure 3.2 shows both the data points from Table 3.1 and the underlying curve. In both year-to-year and regional comparisons, historical variation in effort is used to set up the underlying model for the relationship between costs and results for the category. Whichever comparison is used, the question that needs answering is: What happened to gift response when fund-raising effort was varied in the past?

If a category has no variation in effort over the past several years or over different geographical regions, then the curve cannot be fleshed out. The historical analysis will have less value and may provide only a starting point for later adjustments made through the Delphi process.

As its second objective, the historical analysis needs to provide estimated ranges for the gift levels in each resource allocation category. For example, in the category of individuals

Table 3.1. Sample Direct-Mail Cost-Gift Seven-Year Analysis.
(In thousands of dollars)

Year	Costs	Gift Income
1985	150	2,000
1986	140	1,890
1987	50	300
1988	75	250
1989	100	1,000
1990	120	1,120
1991	110	1,500

Figure 3.2. Sample Direct-Mail Cost-Gift
Data Points with Underlying Curve.

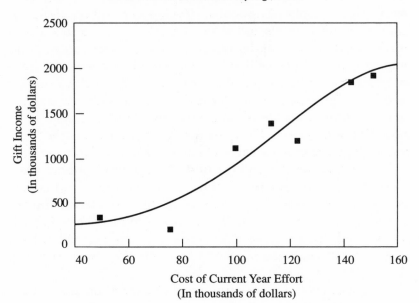

personally solicited for major gifts, how many dollars typically come in each year when very few dollars are expended in the effort? Perhaps the institution cut back on personal solicitation in 1985 to a very low level: how much was pledged that year in major gifts from individuals? This 1985 amount may be used to estimate how many gift dollars would be associated with a zero-level effort. Conversely, what is the maximum level of gifts that has ever come into the category during a campaign when an all-out push was made? This value, adjusted slightly upward, may be a reasonable estimate for the results of maximum effort. A more detailed analysis of the saturation level of each category's market might provide an even better estimate of the maximum-effort response.

The third objective of the historical analysis is to identify carryover effects. The time lapse between solicitation and eventual gift recording needs to be examined for each category to discover whether effort expended in one time period is carried over to another time period. Dollars for the categories with long delays need to be adjusted to reflect the additional costs of raising these gifts. The analysis should uncover the categories where this is a problem. Estimates of the level of carryover come from answering the following question for each category: How much of the current year's gifts are due to effort made in the previous year? If this estimate can be made, the final functional form of the model (described in Chapter Five) will automatically handle the extension to effort going back several years.

Another, simpler way to adjust for carryover is to give more value to gifts from categories with low carryover. Gifts from such short-delay categories are worth more to the institution in comparison with gifts from long-delay categories because the dollars will be available more quickly. In this approach, a carryover estimate is made based on the answer to the following question: How much more is a gift dollar worth in one category than in another, considering the length of time it takes to raise that dollar?

Finally, the fund-raising efforts for some categories may not be associated with the correct results categories, which produces crossover effects. The best example of this at Northwestern University was the fact that the costs for raising corporate matching dollars were connected directly to the annual giving program, but the income was recorded as coming to the corporate category. Other situations—for example, the effect of current direct-mail campaigns on the major-gift programs in later years—are not easily handled because of the potentially long periods of time between expending resources (year after year of direct mail) and receiving the income (years later as a major gift). The analyst should look for any of these crossover effects in the data and report them, even if they may be handled only judgmentally through the Delphi process. In other words, certain market categories can be given more "credit" because of their known influence on securing future gifts from other market categories.

Determination of Fund-Raising Costs

Many different approaches can be used to determine fund-raising costs. The best involve looking at the details of how each staff member spent each hour of his or her day and calculating the costs directly. Since this type of information is rarely kept by a development office, a less accurate approach involves surveying development staff to find out how they allocated their time over the period of the study and then analyzing the budget lines to determine salary costs. The result of this process will be a matrix (stored as an electronic spreadsheet) that has the categories running down the side and the years of the study (or other time period) running across the top. The matrix elements are filled in with the total dollars expended for each category during each time period.

Depending on the institution's requirements, intermediate costs — for example, FTE staff numbers, clerical support, mailing costs, printing costs, and so forth — can be established in the spreadsheet. Graphs can also be produced that show how items such as mailing costs have increased or decreased over the years of the study. Table 3.2 illustrates the basic spreadsheet. (The categories are those described in Chapter Two as ones that could be used in a simple case. They include three techniques — direct mail, phone-a-thon, and personal solicitation — and three markets — individual, corporate, and foundation.)

In many organizations, the budget structure for the development operation may not coincide completely with the categories of programs that are used in the study. For example, at Northwestern, the Planned and Major Gifts Office (PMG) had a budget that associated a cost with the several development officers assigned to work with individuals regarding bequests,

Table 3.2. Sample Fund-Raising Costs Spreadsheet.
(In thousands of dollars)

Allocation Categories	1988	1989	1990	1991	1992
Direct mail	30	32	45	40	35
Phone-a-thon	10	11	23	25	30
Personal-individual	45	50	90	90	95
Personal-corporate	80	85	70	60	60
Personal-foundation	70	75	80	90	100

irrevocable trusts, and outright major gifts. However, school and area development officers also spent some time cultivating and soliciting gifts that overlapped these types. The PMG budget lines in this case did not reflect the allocation of resources to the school and area development staff for raising this kind of gift.

To get around this problem, the officer time devoted to each category can be determined per staff member and then summed to provide an FTE figure for each category. A questionnaire can be developed and sent to development and other key officers, such as the vice president for development and the president of the nonprofit. The president, vice president, and various assistant vice presidents are asked to enter only those FTE numbers reflective of the time spent in direct contact with prospects rather than in administrative tasks.

Occasionally, a staff member holds a position for only part of a year. Perhaps he or she replaced someone no longer at the institution. In this case, several different approaches can be used. A phone call to the former staff member can be made and the questionnaire completed with a short conversation. The supervisor of the former staff member can be asked to estimate the time allocation, or judgments from other peer staff could be used to estimate this data. Because staff turnover can be a problem, an institution may also find it helpful to ask for this data during the exit interview.

In large organizations, consulting the development office telephone directory can ensure the inclusion of all persons who may no longer be employed. If multiple staff directories or telephone lists are produced each year, the one dated as close as possible to the end of the fiscal year (or other reporting period) is used. The directory also is used as the official roster for preparation of the questionnaires. In a decentralized university setting, the alumni relations officers for the various professional schools — for example, medical, law, and business schools — and any regional development officers who are not listed on the central development office telephone list are also sent questionnaires for each appropriate fiscal year.

Among those who will be listed in the directory but who do not need to be sent questionnaires are the professional, technical, and clerical support staff. Professional and technical support staff—for example, research and computer services operations managers—need not be considered in the cost analysis. Secretarial staff salaries, on the other hand, are used in the analysis but their estimate is based on the associated development officer's time allocations. The remaining staff members taken from the telephone lists represent those development officers who were directly involved in the solicitation of gifts from prospects during the years of the study.

The questionnaire should ask the respondents to divide a total of 100 points among the categories, or matrix elements, to show how their time was allocated over the corresponding fiscal year. The points for each matrix element are summed across all responses for each fiscal year in the study. The points are subtotaled separately for associate vice presidents, vice presidents, and presidents so that a different salary multiplier can be used when converting the resulting FTE figure to a dollar value.

An analysis of the budget provides the salary multiplier figure to use for each fiscal year and for certain of the categories or programs. Salary multipliers are determined by averaging those salaries that most accurately represent the category. The management-level multiplier for the associate vice presidential, vice presidential, and presidential level is the average of the salaries at that level regardless of the categories involved. A total professional cost in dollars is determined for each matrix category and each fiscal year by multiplying the FTE for the development officers by the appropriate salary multiplier, and adding to that number the result of multiplying the FTE at the associate vice presidential, vice presidental, and presidential level by the management-level multiplier.

For example, a category consisting of individual prospects who are solicited personally might have 5.6 FTE development officers assigned last year and .5 FTE management-level staff. The average salary for the development officers might be $35,000 per year and the average management-level salary might be $50,000 per year. The professional personnel cost would be $5.6 \times 35,000 + .5 \times 50,000 = \$221,000$.

The only other personnel costs involved are secretarial costs. The ratio of secretarial support to an officer's time usually varies according to the fund-raising technique. Personal solicitation might involve a 1:2 ratio for the time spent, whereas both direct-mail and phone-a-thon programs usually involve additional secretarial support at a 1:1 ratio. Using these figures, secretarial costs can be estimated directly from the FTE figures for each category.

Several other categories of costs might be considered in the analysis: travel expenses, events, publications, mail, telephone, and other typical costs. These figures originate in the budget lines, but in certain cases might need to be distributed across appropriate matrix categories, using the professional FTE numbers to determine the proportions.

For example, suppose the whole development department has a $9,000 annual budget for fund-raising events for all personal solicitation categories (individual, corporate, and foundation). The department has three FTE persons in each of the first two categories (individual and corporate) and one FTE person in the last category (foundation). The proportions are therefore 3/7, 3/7, and 1/7. Multiplying each of these proportions by the $9,000 total results in an individual events cost of $3,857, a corporate events cost of $3,857, and a foundation events cost of $1,286. Obviously, if a department's budget subdivides event costs by category or if the department is small enough to look at the actual event costs, it is better to use the more exact numbers.

All costs are then summed for each matrix element for each fiscal year to provide a grand total development cost. The final result is a comparable cost figure for each cell going back to the first year of the historical analysis.

Determination of Gift Income

Raw aggregate gift income figures are assembled from transactions stored in a computerized data base (or in manual records and reports). Because of the need to relate the gift income to the costs as closely as possible, the analyst must make several adjustments to standard reports that follow the gift accounting practices of organizations such as the Council for Aid and Support of Education (CASE) and the National Association of College and University Business Officers (NACUBO).

First of all, the analyst should consider pledges. Pledge payments should be eliminated from the report and outstanding pledges adjusted to reflect the length of time over which they will be paid, assuming a certain cost of money over the coming years. Think of having to borrow the balance on the pledge throughout the pledge period at some rate. The interest charged during this time must be paid from the pledge payments. Most nonprofits do not borrow against pledges. However, they still need to consider the lost opportunity costs.

The following three examples show how this works. First, a $40,000 pledge paid out over four years of $10,000 payments is only worth $31,699 (assuming a 10 percent cost of borrowing equivalent capital), or only 79 percent of the pledge amount. Second, a $200,000 pledge paid in two $100,000 annual payments is only worth $180,002 (with an 8 percent cost of capital), or only 90 percent of the pledge amount. Third, if the length of the pledge period is unknown, the analyst can assume a typical three-year payout with a 10 percent cost of money and use 80 percent of the pledge amount as a rough estimate for the current value of the pledge. Most spreadsheet programs, such as Lotus 123, provide automatic functions to calculate present values. For example, in Lotus 123 the function is @NPV (interest, range). An adjustment could even be made to reduce the pledges by an expected rate of default, if default is a significant occurrence for an organization. To illustrate this adjustment, the analyst might first reduce a $200,000 pledge to $180,802. Then, because only 70 percent of all pledges are typically ever fulfilled at the organization, the $180,802 is reduced to 70 percent, or $126,561.

Although these adjustments for pledges do help fund raisers associate gift income with the proper year of greatest effort, some may argue that further adjustments also need to be made. Cultivation of individuals, for example, may take place over many years, well before a pledge is finally made. However, in an analysis of the solicitation process at Northwestern University, most of the intense solicitations for particular major gifts from both individuals and nonindividuals occurred within a year of the pledge commitments.

For example, Table 3.3 shows when costs occur in relation to selected gifts in the foundation market at Northwestern. For the selected foundations, all of the pledge payments and their directly related costs were organized by year, with year *t* representing the base year, when the pledges were made. Although there are four years of relatively equal total pledge payments, the costs mainly occurred in the year of the pledge. This finding supports the use of the present value of the pledge commitment and eliminates the need for further pledge adjustments on the report.

The second change to the standard method of recording gifts involves bequests. Bequests cause problems because of the very long delay between the time the gift is solicited and the time it comes to the institution upon the donor's death. Bequests should be handled similarly to pledges. A portion of bequest expectancies should be counted at the time when the bequest is set up and reported to the institution. The amount to be counted can be determined by using an actuarial table. Thirty percent can be used as an estimate in those cases where the exact age of the donor is unknown. This calculation assumes a twenty-year delay and a 10 percent cost of money. When bequests actually come in, they should be eliminated from the current-year gifts reported. Bequests that come in without a prior

Table 3.3. Northwestern University Fund-Raising Costs
and Pledge Payments for Selected Foundations.
(In dollars)

Year	Costs	Pledge Payments
t−3	20	
t−2	650	
t−1	2,278	
t	17,042	140,000
t+1	1,400	157,570
t+2	570	350,935
t+3	230	126,000

bequest expectancy on file should not be counted either, since little direct development effort was probably expended to bring in those particular gifts.

Other gifts not generated by direct development effort can remain in the gift totals only if they have been accounted for in the modeling process. The alternative is to eliminate these transactions from the entire analysis, although it still might be difficult for the Delphi participants to mentally remove these gifts from their predictions of future gift income levels. If the unsolicited gifts are clearly identifiable in the system, the analyst could make notations on the Delphi forms showing the separation and thereby helping the respondents to divide all the gifts into two types: solicited and unsolicited. In most cases, however, this cannot be done.

The third change the analyst must make involves irrevocable trusts. Normally, these gifts are counted at their total market value at the time the trust is set up. This number should be adjusted to reflect the gift's true value to the institution. This can be a difficult task, since the gift may set up an annuity trust that will pay an income stream to several people over each of their lifetimes. At Northwestern, we recently gained control of the principal of an annuity trust that was set up over forty years ago. To have correctly estimated the true cash value in the 1940s would have been nearly impossible. One approach, in those cases where it is difficult to determine a value, is to use the best judgment of the organization's accounting staff. In difficult cases, a certain percent of total market value — for example, 50 percent — might be agreed to by all parties involved.

Once the donor or other specified individual dies, the dollars which created the annuity trust are made available to the nonprofit. However, these funds must not be double counted as gifts when they are finally accessible to the nonprofit organization. If the nonprofit is the trustee of the trust, double counting is usually not a problem. In this case, the funds will have been recorded by the nonprofit's accounting department when the gift was originally given. When the nonprofit is not the trustee, only the beneficiary, a bank is usually the trustee. In this case, the development office may have originally counted the gift when notified of the trust's existence, but the accounting department may not have recorded it. When the principle is released to the nonprofit, the accounting department will count the money—but the development office should not count the money a second time (even if the value has increased over the years).

After making these three adjustments to pledges, bequests, and irrevocable trusts, the analyst determines the totals by category, going back several years. Most institutions have computer systems that can be programmed to produce the proper results. However, some categories may not be easily identifiable in the system. For example, direct-mail and phone-a-thon gifts may not be distinguishable in the computer system (solicitation coding). In this case, it may be necessary to sample the gift transactions and look in the manual backup files to discover how the gifts were solicited. (In addition, the system should be reprogrammed to track and store solicitation codes from this time forward.)

What is usually more problematic is the determination of gifts that were solicited personally instead of by other means. For example, a donor could have been visited several times over a three-year period by a regional officer seeking a major gift. After the third visit, the prospect writes a check, but sends it back in a direct-mail business reply envelope. The gift-processing staff inadvertently records this as a direct-mail gift. Or perhaps the donor is the American Cancer Society, supporting research in a medical school. All of the contact involved in getting the grants was made by the medical school faculty, and the cost of this contact was not counted in the direct fund-raising costs. Does the computer system record a distinction for these transactions? Certainly each institution will have different problems in correctly assigning gifts to the various categories. A look at a sample of transactions is recommended in order to find the problems. If the sample is large enough, it can be used to establish a reasonable estimate of giving by category for the historical analysis.

Compilation of the Minimum Aggregate Results

After completing the minimum aggregate historical analysis, the analyst determines the following data for each allocation category:

1. Total costs for the category for each of the past three to six years.
2. Total adjusted gifts received through the category for each of the past three to six years.
3. An estimate of the level of gift income that would come in through each category with very little or no development effort.
4. An estimate of the level of gift income that would come in through each category with an all-out development effort.
5. Identification of category crossover, where effort in one category affects the resulting gifts in another category.
6. Identification of extensive carryover effect, where efforts from past years affect the current year's results.

Tables 3.4, 3.5, and 3.6 illustrate how these data might be recorded for a typical nonprofit fund-raising operation.

Compilation of a Detailed Analysis

Beyond the minimum level of analysis, a detailed analysis of development activities and gifts can provide insight into the ways development efforts affect eventual gift income. A detailed analysis is performed by selecting representative prospects from each category and looking at the particular development efforts carried out and the particular gifts received. The detailed effort, pledge, and gift transactions for a group of prospects from each category are coded into computer transactions for this examination.

Table 3.4. Historical Analysis of Sample Costs and Gifts.
(In thousands of dollars)

Category	1988	1989	Costs/Gifts 1990	1991	1992
Direct mail	30/250	32/270	45/500	40/350	35/400
Phone-a-thon	10/100	11/150	23/300	25/350	30/300
Personal-individual	45/1,000	50/1,200	90/1,100	90/1,200	95/3,010
Personal-corporate	80/500	85/550	70/550	60/400	60/450
Personal-foundation	70/400	75/350	80/800	90/700	100/900

Table 3.5. Historical Analysis of Development Costs.
(In thousands of dollars)

Category	Low-Development-Cost Gift Level	High-Development-Cost Gift Level
Direct mail	10	1,200
Phone-a-thon	5	750
Personal-individual	20	5,000
Personal-corporate	50	1,500
Personal-foundation	60	2,500

Table 3.6. Historical Analysis of
Crossover and Carryover Effects.

Category	Crossover Effects	Carryover Effects
Direct mail	Affects personal-individual	Very little
Phone-a-thon	Affects personal-individual	Very little
Personal-individual	Affected by direct mail Affected by phone-a-thon Affects personal-corporate	Very much
Personal-corporate	Affected by personal-individual	Much
Personal-foundation	None	Much

In particular, time delays between fund-raising efforts and gifts should be noted. Statistical regression analysis can be performed to determine the delay effect down to the month level. (A full description of this kind of analysis and the results from the Northwestern University study can be found in Lindahl, 1990.)

An initial historical analysis need not go into great detail. The minimum information needed in the historical analysis of fund-raising operation consists of the aggregate costs and benefits in each category or program (Table 3.4), an estimate of the level of gifts that might arrive in a category with both very little and very great development effort (Table 3.5), and the identification of carryover and crossover effects (Table 3.6). Beyond these aggregate numbers and relationships, extensive detailed analysis can be used to help development staff further understand how development effort and resource allocation affect the gift income stream.

4

Bringing Out
Staff Expertise
in a Strategic Planning
Session

The strategic planning session, scheduled after year-end fund-raising results are known and before the budget is set for the coming year, provides the forum for the setting of the mission statement, the discussion of various strategies, and the development of a workable budget plan for the coming year. As mentioned earlier, ideally this session is held over two days—preferably at a location away from the office.

Attending this session, or retreat, should be all development officers (or a representative group for large development offices), the person in charge of allocating fund-raising resources, and in smaller nonprofits, key persons from outside the development office, such as the head of the organization and the chairperson of the board of directors. The main objective is to include both those persons who will sign off on the budget plan and those who have the greatest knowledge about the responsiveness of each allocation category to changes in the fund-raising effort. However, this group should also be limited to around twenty persons to facilitate discussion in the Delphi process.

A typical agenda for a two-day planning retreat appears in Exhibit 4.1. This agenda is only one example of how the strategic planning session could be structured. However, any change should still allow time for the analyst to prepare a report for the second day. The order of events in the sample agenda will structure the remainder of the discussion in this chapter.

Exhibit 4.1. Two-Day Retreat Agenda.

Day One

    Discussion of mission and determination of prioritization multiplier for allocation categories.

    Discussion of issues affecting response of markets: taxes, internal organization changes, historical analysis, and external conditions. (In subsequent years, a comparison between expected and actual gifts would be reviewed as a part of the historical analysis.)

Lunch

    Delphi Round One

        Discussion of possible funding scenarios for each category.

        Completion of round one Delphi surveys by each person individually.

Dinner

    Analyst prepares graphical report from round one surveys.

Day Two

    Delphi Round Two

        Discussion of results of round one Delphi surveys.

        Completion of round two Delphi surveys by each person individually.

Lunch

    Closing.

Mission Statement and Multipliers

Determining the mission of the fund-raising office of a nonprofit organization is much simpler than determining the mission of the organization itself. Certainly the fund-raising operation's main focus is bringing in financial resources for the nonprofit organization. However, it can be helpful to fine tune the statement of purpose regarding the scope of interaction with various potential markets — for example, private sources versus public sources — and in regard to the prioritization of certain gifts over others — for example, unrestricted versus restricted gifts. The desired level of donor participation and other factors important to the particular nonprofit should also be discussed.

Although the mission of the entire organization will not be discussed directly in this process, it is crucial to recall that mission. If the organization has a mission statement prepared, it could be read to the group or passed out for reading ahead of time. Any fund-raising mission statement produced during this process must tie back to the organization's mission statement.

Leading the mission statement discussion can be difficult because of the many potential sidetracks. Each of the open-ended questions mentioned in Chapter One could generate a lengthy discussion. The initial work done by the steering committee to establish allocation categories can be useful in organizing the discussion. What is it about a certain program, direct mail for example, that supports a certain aspect of the mission beyond simply raising dollars? Direct mail provides high participation levels but low dollar amounts. It provides cash in the current year instead of the next five to ten years, and most of this cash is for unrestricted purposes. Each category should be similarly evaluated for particular values related to the development operation's mission. To record the results of the discussion, an overhead projector could be set up with a transparency containing a list of the categories. Each category's possible benefits, beyond the simple dollar value of the gifts it produces, can then be written in on the transparency.

Four of the more typical value-added benefits for many nonprofits are priority, the value of the gift in terms of how closely its purpose meets the high-priority needs of the nonprofit; public relations, the value of the gift insofar as it changes the organization's public image; related contacts, the value of additional gifts received by the institution because of another donor's contacts and connections; and long-term giving, the added value of a gift because of the high probability of a long-lasting stream of additional gifts.

Table 4.1 shows what the overhead transparency might look like using these four areas. The high, medium, and low scores represent the consensus of the group regarding how well gifts from each category provide each specific benefit.

Once the overhead is filled in for each category, as in Table 4.1, a combined rating is given to each category. This can be done by averaging the scores for each of the four benefit areas, by selecting the middle score, or by picking the most frequent score. If some of the four areas of added value happen to support the mission more closely than the others, a weighted average could be used. The scores in the more important areas would be worth correspondingly higher amounts. A high score in the first column might be worth six points, while a high score in the second column might be worth only three points. In Table 4.2, the combined score was developed by simple averaging of the scores in Table 4.1 (high = 3, medium = 2, low = 1), under the assumption that each added value supported the mission equally well. For the phone-a-thon category, for example, the scores in Table 4.1 were translated to a numerical value: priority = 3, high; public relations = 2, medium; related contacts =

Table 4.1. Sample Consensus on Added Value.

Category	Priority	Public Relations	Related Contacts	Long-Term Giving
Direct mail	high	low	low	high
Phone-a-thon	high	medium	high	high
Personal-individual	low	high	medium	medium
Personal-foundation	low	medium	low	high
Personal-corporate	low	low	low	low

Table 4.2. Sample Combined Added-Value Scores.

Category	Combined Points	Combined Score
Direct mail	3 + 1 + 1 + 3	8/4 = 2 (medium)
Phone-a-thon	3 + 2 + 3 + 3	11/4 = 2.75 (high)
Personal-individual	1 + 3 + 2 + 2	8/4 = 2 (medium)
Personal-foundation	1 + 2 + 1 + 3	7/4 = 1.75 (medium)
Personal-corporate	1 + 1 + 1 + 1	4/4 = 1 (low)

3, high; and long-term giving = 3, high. These values were then averaged $(3 + 2 + 3 + 3)/4 = 2.75$.

Ranking the categories by their average scores shows how closely each one reflects the true mission of the fund-raising office. In the example, the order, from most to least valuable, is (1) phone-a-thon, (2) personal-individual, (3) direct mail, (4) personal-foundation, (5) personal-corporate.

Finally, an estimate of the dollar value of the benefits needs to be determined. If the original dollar value is $1.00, how many additional cents would the highest level of additional benefits be worth? Suppose by consensus (or average of the participants' votes), the top additional value is estimated to be $.50 beyond the $1.00 cash value. Then the top category would be credited with $1.50 for each $1.00 in gifts. In Table 4.2, that would be the phone-a-thon program. The following category, personal-individual, would be credited with proportionately less per cash dollar (perhaps $1.40 for each $1.00). Gifts from the lowest category (personal-corporate) would be credited with only $1.10 for each $1.00 in cash gifts.

These added values, $1.50 through $1.10, are referred to as multipliers, since they will be multiplied against the total gift figure for each category later, during the optimization process described in Chapter Six. They are a quantifiable way to represent the greater value of gifts from categories that are closer to the mission of the fund-raising operation. Multipliers allow the mission to be factored into quantitative comparisons across programs. In this way, more valuable programs will receive greater allocations.

At Northwestern University, the assignment of multiplier values and the ranking of categories was done via a survey sent out to development and central administration staff before the strategic planning session. Using these responses, a somewhat complex method of assigning multiplier values was established. But, essentially, the method was a variation on the weighted-average process described here.

Table 4.3 indicates the combined scores and multipliers given for each of the categories. For example, looking at the second category (alumni-personal-annual, or APA) the combined points show that gifts in this category are next to the top in terms of added value—in this example, *lower* points are better; a category with a score of 52 is worse than 46, but better than 57. The multiplier of $1.435 means that every $1.00 in gifts attributed to the APA category will be multiplied by $1.435 in the optimization process in order to reflect the added value.

Table 4.3. Northwestern University Added-Value Multiplier.

Category (market-technique-gift type)	Combined Points (Lower points are better)	Multiplier
Alumni-personal-major	46	$1.500
Alumni-personal-annual	52	1.435
Corporate-personal-major	57	1.380
Alumni-personal-irrevocable	60	1.348
Foundation-personal-major	62	1.326
Nonalumni-personal-major	62	1.326
Corporate-personal-annual	63	1.315
Alumni-personal-bequest	64	1.304
Alumni–phone-a-thon–annual	64	1.304
Alumni–direct mail–annual	67	1.272
Nonalumni-personal-annual	68	1.261
Parents-personal-major	70	1.239
Nonalumni-personal-irrevocable	76	1.174
Parents-personal-annual	77	1.163
Nonalumni-personal-bequest	80	1.130
Parents–direct mail–annual	92	1.000

Issues Affecting Response of Markets

Taxes, internal organizational changes, historical analysis, and external conditions are just some of the topics that could be discussed in the planning session. Depending on the extent of the historical analysis, a review of the results could take up much of the time. However, this information could also be printed ahead of time and distributed for evening reading before the second day's discussion. Certainly, if the three tables that make up the minimum aggregate results (described in Chapter Three) represent the extent of the analysis, the review of the materials will not take very long. During this review process, it is important that the participants clearly understand the results, since the historical information will be integrated into the second round of the Delphi process.

Experts on different issues, such as taxes, should be asked to give summaries that focus on how these issues may affect the preset allocation categories. The subsequent discussion could then focus on whether the development officers active in each field agree or disagree on the suggested effects.

Although the true purpose of this part of the session is to further inform the Delphi participants, the group might be inclined to try to quantify the environmental effects. To do this, a multiplier that quantifies the effect the environment has on responsiveness to a fund-raising effort is set up for each allocation category. For example, tax law changes may make direct-mail gifts, which are typically small ones, more beneficial to the donor, as the 1986 tax law changes did when they allowed people who did not itemize to deduct charitable contributions. If the participants agree on this effect, a multiplier of $1.20 could be set up to boost the level of projected response. Each $1.00 in gifts from the direct-mail category would be boosted to $1.20 (above and beyond the effect of the added-value multiplier described earlier). Or, if corporations are in a deep recession, a multiplier of $.80 could be used to reduce the effect of effort in this area when considered against past efforts.

Using the nonquantified approach, each participant simply takes the environmental factors into account when judging how development effort affects market response. After discussing any tax law changes and the current economic conditions, participants mentally reduce (or increase) the expected level of response, as established by the historical levels, by the amount they believe will be accurate.

The morning session closes with the group developing a true sense of mission, understanding how the allocation categories relate back to the mission statement, learning about past historical successes or failures for each of the categories, and sharing the best expert opinions as to the effect of the internal and external environment on the expected response of each program to development effort. They are now prepared to begin the formal Delphi process after the lunch break.

Delphi Round One

The Delphi session begins with the retreat leader passing out a response sheet packet to each participant. The packets contain one sheet for each allocation category. Figure 4.1 shows a sample response sheet for the category of personally solicited major gifts from individuals. On each sheet, there are five columns or graphical bars. Each column will represent a range of gift income responses to a particular funding scenario. These columns are left blank to be completed by the participants. The center column represents the income for the category's base-case or previous-year funding level. The two columns to the right represent scenarios with slightly more and much more funding effort than the base case, while the two columns to the left represent slightly less and much less funding effort than the base case. The base-case funding allocation level is already filled in on the sheets.

In the upper right hand corner of the sheet, the number of the round (either 1 or 2) and the name of respondent are recorded. The five vertical columns can be thought of as forming a bar chart with each bar representing a different level of funding. The bar to the left represents the least amount of funding (large decrease), while the bar to the far right represents the greatest level of funding (large increase). The height of each

Figure 4.1. Sample Delphi Round One Response Sheet.

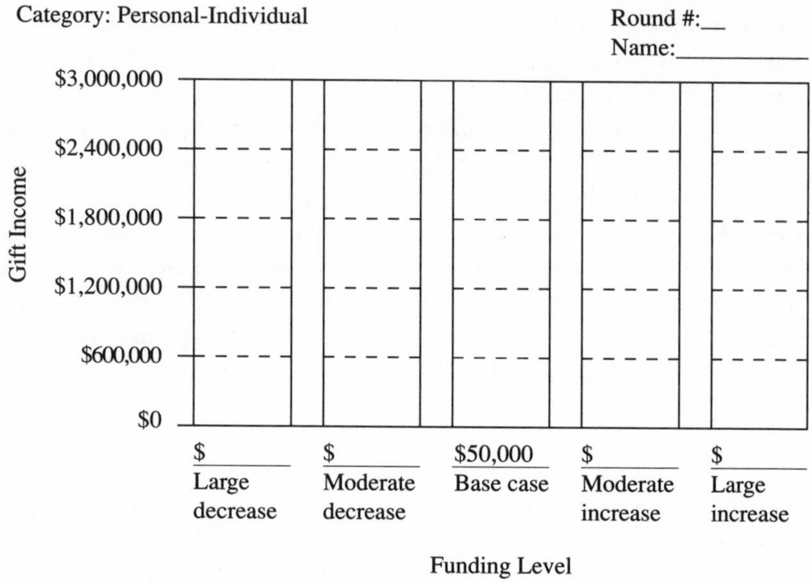

Category: Personal-Individual   Round #:__
                                                                 Name:_____

bar represents the expected level of gifts for the corresponding level of funding.

The response sheets may also have areas that record estimates of two other variables that may be used in more sophisticated analyses. The first variable is the level at which gifts would be expected to come in without any fund-raising effort. This is a difficult variable to estimate, since some effort has usually been allocated throughout the recent past. The second variable is the amount of gifts coming in this year that are due to effort in the previous year (carryover). Once again, this variable is difficult to estimate, although a detailed historical analysis may reveal a good starting amount. This variable is important for some long-term programs and must be estimated if the final strategy is to optimize results over more than the coming year. Since the inclusion of these two variables adds to the complexity of the process, nonprofits may opt to ignore them in the first year of strategic planning and then incorporate them into the second or third year of planning.

After taking a few minutes to describe the sheets, the retreat leader begins a discussion of the appropriate funding levels for each category. (It may be useful to make a tape recording of this discussion for use in later analysis.) The leader might begin by asking: What would a category's program manager do with an additional amount of resources? What would the manager do with less than the current amount? In discussing a phone-a-thon program, for example, session participants might want to consider increasing the coverage from three nights to four nights of trying to reach each prospect. What would this cost? Or perhaps the program should simply use better calling techniques — for example, a newly developed training program funded by a resource allocation increase. Perhaps the program should switch to paid callers instead of volunteers. Then, the participants should consider the effects of decreases in effort. Perhaps the calling pool could be reduced and only past donors called. Or, if the program switched from paid to volunteer callers, would that cause a large decrease in response level?

After the discussion, the participants must agree on the amounts to assign to the four levels of possible funding (large decrease, moderate decrease, moderate increase, large increase) for each category, but they do not necessarily have to agree on particular ways of spending the increases or decreases. The discussion also serves to inform those development officers that have little familiarity with a particular program, so that they get a feel for how changes in resources will affect the type of program that can be implemented. They will be better able to predict response levels for unfamiliar programs and to serve as skeptics whenever experts' projections appear unreasonable.

Once the participants reach a consensus about the levels, the amounts are written onto each sheet. Following a break, the Delphi participants complete the sheets confidentially, marking their predicted gift income for each of the categories' five funding levels by drawing a bar across the column at the projected income level. They may use data from the historical analysis and from any discussion about the environment — but they must not talk to each other. Any questions must be referred to the session leader. Procedural issues should be clarified to the whole group as they come up, so that everyone interprets the sheets consistently. A participant who considers himself or herself an expert in a particular category should mark that response sheet "Expert." The expert's predicted gift levels will be flagged on the round one summary sheet for the benefit of participants in the next round.

Analysis of Delphi Round One

After the sheets are collected, the analyst puts together the materials for the second round of the Delphi process. A summary sheet for each category needs to be assembled by recording the marks from each participant's sheets. Transferring these marks is a relatively fast and uncomplicated process. Expert's marks are noted by placing an "E" next to the mark.

Historical estimates of income for each level of funding are also added to the summary sheets. In the example I have been using (Table 3.4), the personal-individual category had historical costs/gifts as follows (in thousands of dollars): 45/1,000, 50/1,200, 90/1,100, 90/1,200 and 95/3,010. The analyst graphs these data points and draws the underlying curves. For each of the possible funding levels established by the Delphi participants, the corresponding gift values are recorded from the curve (also in thousands of dollars): 20/800, 40/900, 50/1,200, 60/1,300, 100/2,700. These historical levels are flagged with an "H" on each bar, and they provide guideposts for the respondents as they judge the future responsiveness of the personal-individual category to development effort.

The final results might look like the sample summary sheet shown in Figure 4.2. The suggested funding levels have been filled in across the bottom of the sheet. A line has been drawn on each column for each respondent's estimate of the gift income that will result from the corresponding funding amount. Lines with an "E" are experts' estimates, and lines with an "H" indicate predicted gift levels based solely on the historical analysis.

Using this graphical representation of the summary results, the participants can easily relate their responses to other

Figure 4.2. Sample Delphi Round One Summary Sheet.

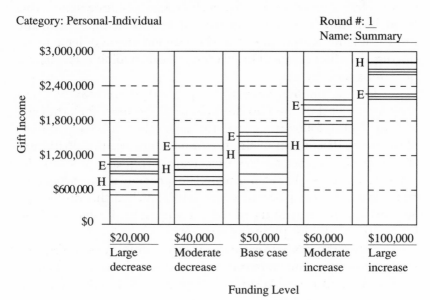

Category: Personal-Individual

Round #: 1
Name: Summary

participants' responses. When a summary sheet is set for each category, packets are produced for each participant, consisting of a copy of the summary and a new set of response sheets, one for each category. The new sheets, however, have all five levels of funding written across the bottom.

Delphi Round Two

The second round of the Delphi process begins with an extensive discussion of the results from the first round. Those individuals who predicted gift levels well below or above the others are asked to explain why they saw responses that were so dramatically different from everyone else's. Experts are also asked to explain their answers. Extensive and lively discussions usually ensue as development officers defend their predictions with detailed explanations of how the markets will respond to different levels of fund-raising effort.

After the discussion and a break, each participant is asked to complete a second sheet for each category. Once again, this is an individual process, and the materials available are the historical analysis and any notes the respondents may have made during the discussion. The leader is also available to answer questions as they come up.

During the first year of this process, there may be extra time at the end of the two days that can be used for other activities. In the following years, the schedule can be adjusted to allow more discussion of the previous year's results. What are the reasons for the success of certain programs beyond the predicted values? What happened to prevent some programs from achieving the planned result levels? When this discussion is added at the beginning of the retreat, the full two days will be required for the planning session.

After the staff members return from the session, the analyst puts together a summary sheet for the second Delphi round. Second-round results (Figure 4.3) will look similar to

Figure 4.3. Sample Delphi Round Two Summary Sheet.

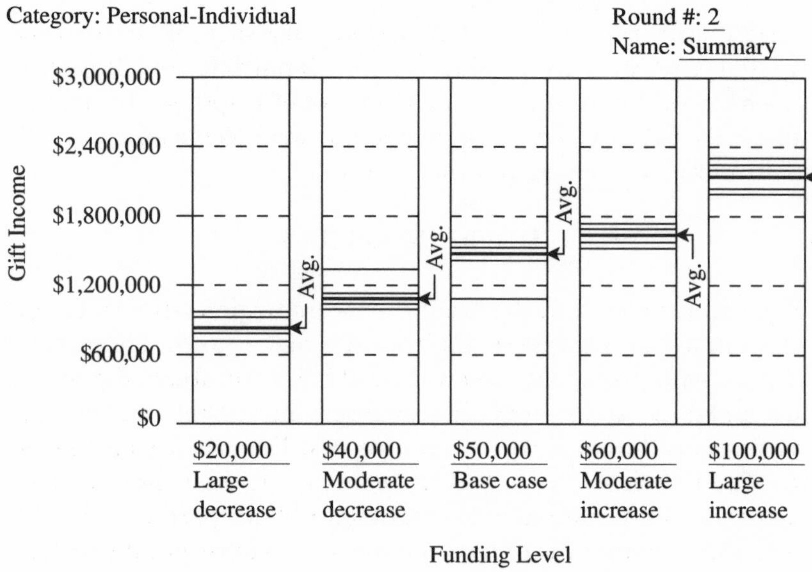

Category: Personal-Individual

Round #: 2
Name: Summary

the first-round results, except that an average predicted level will be determined for each funding scenario and each category on the second summary. This can be done visually, by looking for the "middle" of the responses, or analytically, by using non-linear regression to determine the underlying curve (Chapter Five will describe this process). A bold line in each column indicates the average response for that funding level, and historical and expert indicators are not used. Finally, the completed summary sheet is sent to all respondents.

5

Building
a Predictive Model

After the Delphi process is completed and the results that predict the gift income for each category's five potential funding levels are available, the analyst must develop an appropriate model to be used in the optimization process. The model will be a mathematical representation that tries to mirror the reality of the relationship between costs and gifts. To predict how a system will react to a change in funding level, development officers look to the model to see how it reacts. The model described in this chapter is "calibrated" with the guidance of both historical experience and staff judgments. Because of this, staff will be confident that the model comes as close as possible to reflecting reality.

A Simple Model

There are two approaches that can be taken to develop a model, depending on the sophistication desired. The first approach uses the visually determined average values for each funding level and each category to define the model. In this approach, the Delphi results provide a model directly. Figure 5.1 illustrates a Delphi summary sheet that is ready to be used to build a model. The values that correspond to the "average" lines shown on the summary sheet are recorded in a table that includes the averages from all the allocation categories. A sample table with four categories, direct mail, phone-a-thon, personal-individual, and personal-nonindividual is shown in Table 5.1. It sets out the funding level and expected gift income of each category for the coming year. The numbers in Table 5.1 provide an estimate for each possible funding level, and this kind of table can be used in an optimization process to determine the best resource allocations for the coming year.

A visual determination of the average Delphi responses will probably suffice for most nonprofits just beginning to use this strategic planning process. Moreover, sticking to these five funding levels will always provide an implementable resource

Figure 5.1. Delphi Summary Sheet for Model Building.

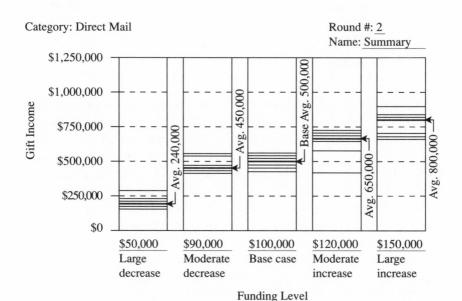

Table 5.1. Funding Level and Expected Gift Income.
(In dollars)

Category	Funding Level	Gift Income
Direct mail		
Large decrease	50,000	240,000
Moderate decrease	90,000	450,000
Base case	100,000	500,000
Moderate increase	120,000	650,000
Large increase	150,000	800,000
Phone-a-thon		
Large decrease	10,000	20,000
Moderate decrease	20,000	50,000
Base case	30,000	60,000
Moderate increase	40,000	75,000
Large increase	85,000	150,000
Personal-individual		
Large decrease	20,000	100,000
Moderate decrease	40,000	600,000
Base case	65,000	700,000
Moderate increase	90,000	900,000
Large increase	150,000	1,000,000
Personal-nonindividual		
Large decrease	20,000	300,000
Moderate decrease	40,000	350,000
Base case	50,000	400,000
Moderate increase	80,000	500,000
Large increase	100,000	550,000

allocation strategy. However, a better average can be determined with just a bit more effort and expertise by using a software package such as SAS or SPSS. Furthermore, the model that comes directly from the Delphi summary lacks gift income estimates in between the five selected funding levels. What if a funding level that fell between two of the selected funding levels were really better than either of the other two? It is helpful to have a model that considers broad levels of funding beyond the five provided in the Delphi summary. The following section describes how to set up a model that has a predicted gift income for all possible funding levels. Readers who are planning to use the simple model may skip the following section.

A Continuous Model

In order to use a statistical routine (nonlinear regression) to determine the continuous effort response functions for each allocation category, a general form of the function must be hypothesized. In other words, what is the general relationship between funding and gifts? As mentioned earlier, Paton (1986) and Steinberg (1985) discuss what such a relationship might look like.

Both Paton and Steinberg show a model that begins with some level of gift income coming in without much cost. At first, as the effort increases, the gift income stays stable due to the high cost of setting up a fund-raising program. However, after a certain threshold is reached, the curve moves up sharply, reflecting the program's efficiency. However, beyond a certain point, the capacity and interest of the market reach saturation and the curve levels out. As I illustrated in Chapter Three (see Figures 3.1 and 3.2), any increase in funding now will produce little if any growth in gift revenue.

The general form of the curve for a standard sales response function is similar to the curve described here and in Figures 3.1 and 3.2. The specific version of the function used is the same that ZS Associates (a consulting firm that specializes in sales force allocation) has used for many years in modeling the sales force allocation problem. This mathematical model states that for each category, the upcoming year's gift income is a combination of three values: (1) no-effort gifts, (2) gifts coming from effort of past years, and (3) current-effort gifts. The general response function takes the form:

$$Y_t = a + b(Y_{t-1} - a) + d(X_t^g / (X_t^g + c))$$

where terms are defined as follows:

Y_t is the total gift dollars predicted to come into the nonprofit in year t. (This value is adjusted for the payments that will come in future years for commitments made in year t. A 10 percent interest factor could be used to determine the current value of these future payments.)

> a represents those dollars received in year t that are not
> solicited by development or that have very small costs
> associated with the corresponding solicitation stream
> in any year (t or earlier).
>
> Y_{t-1} is the total gift dollars for year t-1. (These values are
> adjusted for the current-year benefits of future-year
> pledge payments.)
>
> b represents the carryover rate from the solicitation effort
> from previous years that is not directly associated with
> the proactive solicitation streams of the current year.
>
> d represents the maximum proactive gift dollars raised
> during the year t beyond those dollars that are not
> solicited (a) or attributed to past years' efforts ($b(Y_{t-1} -$
> $a)$).
>
> X_t is the development costs for the year t, including both
> proactive and stewardship costs.
>
> g is a constant that relates to the quickness of the rise in
> the function.
>
> c is a constant that also relates to the rate of increase of
> the function (used as a competition term in the sales
> model).
>
> $(X_t^g/(X_t^g + c))$ is a fraction between 0 and 1 which indicates
> what portion of d is being actualized during the year t.

Figure 5.2 uses an example from Northwestern University to illustrate these various parameters as they are used in the response curve.

To determine the specific functions for each category, the analyst first develops values for constants a (the level of no-effort gifts) and b (the rate of carryover). Both of these values were estimated by the Delphi participants, so there will be up to twenty different estimates for each parameter. The median number might be good to use here, but better yet, the historical analysis could also be used to help determine more realistic numbers. For a, the development officers might be likely to underestimate how many gifts would come in without any of their efforts. For b, the development officers might overestimate

Figure 5.2. Northwestern University Alumni-
Personal-Irrevocable Response Curve.

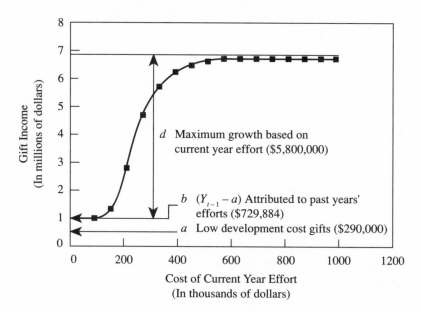

the effects from last year on this year's results. How the analyst combines the Delphi results and the historical analysis will vary from case to case, but the two parameters must be estimated for each category.

Armed with estimates for a and b, along with the gift income levels from the previous year (Y_{t-1}), only g, c, and d are left to determine. This is done using any nonlinear regression program like SAS or SPSS. Data points (X, Y) for each category consist of the responses from each Delphi respondent. If twenty people participated in the Delphi process, then for each category there would be 20 (people) × 5 (funding levels) = 100 data points. The SAS program shown in Exhibit 5.1 illustrates how the problem was set up for Northwestern for one of the categories. The program could easily be converted for other institutions.

Once the parameters are set, the model, with a function for each category, is ready to be used in the optimization process.

Exhibit 5.1. Sample SAS Program.

```
TITLE 'MODEL PARAMETERS-ALUMNI/DIRECT MAIL/ANNUAL GIFTS'
DATA file;
INPUT X Y;
CARDS;
data1 data2
. . . . . . . .
;
PROC NLIN
     MAXITER = 200 ;
PARMS D = 4984811                                    (starting values)
      G = 2.92
      C = 7.9e16
BOUNDS 0 < G < 5,  3000000 < D < 6000000,  C > 0;
MODEL Y = 126744 + D*((X**G)/((X**G) + C));
```

Graphs of the function for each category should also be produced for the development officers so they can use them to visualize how their efforts might affect gift income (see Figure 5.2). After the model is set up, the next step is to determine each category's optimal resource allocation — that is, the allocation that will get the greatest gift revenue for the organization.

Three of Northwestern University's formula statements provide some final examples of model building. Note that each formula statement follows the form of the general response function described earlier. Various priority multipliers were used with each function to produce the final form.

Alumni-personal-annual (APA):

$$Y_{apat} = 500,000 + .05 \ (Y_{apat-1} - 500,000) +$$
$$3,719,008 \ (X_{apat}^{.938262779}/(X_{apat}^{.938262779} + 333,318.461))$$

Alumni-personal-irrevocable trusts (API):

$$Y_{apit} = 250,000 + .15 \ (Y_{apit-1} - 250,000) +$$
$$12,987,607(X_{apit}^{1.077488168}/(X_{apit}^{1.077488168} + 1,333,348.164))$$

Alumni-phon-a-thon (major and annual) (AHA):

$$Y_{ahat} = .05 \ (Y_{ahat-1}) +$$
$$2,404,052 \ (X_{ahat}^{1.329523678}/(X_{ahat}^{1.329523678} + 28,548,779))$$

6

Devising
a Strategy
That Optimizes
Fund-Raising Income

Optimization refers to the process of looking at all possible combinations of funding levels for the various categories to determine which combination will make the net adjusted gift income the highest. When the number of combinations is very small, development officers can tell just by looking which is best. As the choices mount, a computer can be used to check out hundreds, thousands, or even millions of combinations in a relatively short time.

Bear in mind that the optimal solution of a mathematical model is really only an educated guess at the true optimal solution. Based on the historical analysis and the judgmental data from Delphi respondents, the model can only be as good as the estimates provided. The optimization process is only a tool that takes the best estimates for the responsiveness of each category and reveals the best resource allocation given these estimates. Nevertheless, this approach is a step beyond using unstructured intuition or considering the cost per dollar raised.

When the cost per dollar raised is used, the problem of marginal, or next dollar, rates, described in Chapter One, can cause faulty allocation strategies. The implicit assumption is that the cost per dollar raised will stay constant as additional dollars are allocated, but this ignores how saturated a particular market may have become. The example that follows demonstrates the difference in allocation strategies when using the cost per dollar raised versus the optimization techniques outlined in this book.

Simple Model Approach

The model-building process described in Chapter Five sets the stage for the optimization process. If the simple approach was used in creating a model, then optimization can be accomplished using a spreadsheet program such as Lotus 123. The cells are filled with the various levels of funding for each category and the estimated net total gifts. The sort program is used to rank the alternatives.

More specifically, the following columns should be set up for each scenario, or set of funding alternatives, within each category:

> Scenario number
> Cat1 costs
> Cat1 gifts
> . . .
>
> CatN costs
> CatN gifts
> Cat1 adj mult
> Cat1 adj gifts
> . . .
>
> CatN adj mult
> CatN adj gifts
> Total costs
> Tot adj gifts

The column headings have the following meanings:

> *The scenario number* helps staff to keep track of each scenario and to reset the spreadsheet after sorting. This number runs from 1 to the total number of possible scenarios.

> *Cat1 costs* is the year cost to the institution for the fund-raising activity in category 1 (DM, or direct mail, in the example shown in Table 6.1). The heading in the actual spreadsheet should name each category in Cat1 through CatN to prevent confusion. N, of course, is the total number of categories.

> *Cat1 gifts* is the estimated yearly amount of gift income coming in from the fund-raising effort in category 1. This number should already have been adjusted by the process described earlier — for example, pledge payments have been removed and outstanding pledges have been included at a reduced value. This number should represent, to the best of the analyst's ability, the current year's results.

> *Cat1 adj mult* is used when multipliers have been set up in the mission section of the strategic planning session. Multiplier values set up in this column will range around the $1.00 mark (which represents no adjustment). The spreadsheet will use this number in calculating the next column.

> *Cat1 adj gifts* is used to determine the total gifts to optimize. To calculate this value for each scenario, multiply cat1 gifts by the multiplier cat1 adj mult and subtract cat1 costs, the cost of raising these dollars: Cat1 adj gifts = (Cat1 gifts × Cat1 adj mult) − Cat1 costs. This value will represent the projected net dollars raised through the first category's fund-raising program.

Total costs is the sum of costs in all categories.

Tot adj gifts is the sum of adjusted gifts for each
category. It is the number that will be optimized
by selecting the best scenario.

Table 6.1 is an example of a spreadsheet set up for four
categories: DM (direct mail), PH (phon-a-thon), PI (personally
raised individual gifts), PN (personally raised nonindividual
gifts).
Notice the pattern in the noncalculated fields (category
costs, category gifts, and multipliers). Some skillful "cutting and
pasting" in Lotus 123 can simplify the data entry process. Otherwise, the analyst needs to enter each possible combination of
funding levels. For three to five categories, the entry is not too
time consuming ($5 \times 5 \times 5 = 125$ up to $5 \times 5 \times 5 \times 5 \times 5 = 3,125$).
For greater numbers of categories, the use of additional as-

Table 6.1. Four-Category Funding Scenarios.[a]
(In thousands of dollars)

Scenario number	1	2	3	. . .	625
DM costs	50	50	50	. . .	150
DM gifts	240	240	240	. . .	800
PH costs	10	10	10	. . .	85
PH gifts	20	20	20	. . .	150
PI costs	20	20	20	. . .	150
PI gifts	100	100	100	. . .	1,000
PN costs	20	40	50	. . .	100
PN gifts	300	350	400	. . .	900
DM adj mult	1.05	1.05	1.05	. . .	1.05
DM adj gifts	252	252	252	. . .	840
PH adj mult	1.08	1.08	1.08	. . .	1.08
PH adj gifts	21.6	21.6	21.6	. . .	162
PI adj mult	1.1	1.1	1.1	. . .	1.1
PI adj gifts	110	110	110	. . .	1,100
PN adj mult	.95	.95	.95	. .	.95
PN adj gifts	285	332.5	380	. . .	855
Total costs	100	120	130	. . .	485
Total adj gifts	668.6	716.1	763.6	. . .	2,957

[a]Change row headings to column headings when setting up the spreadsheet.

sistance should be considered—either internally, by hiring a programmer to write an optimization routine (essentially mimicking the spreadsheet process), or externally, through contracting with a consulting firm.

Once all the scenarios are entered into the spreadsheet, the optimization process is rather simple. Each spreadsheet package will have a different command for sorting. In Lotus, the data/sort command is used to sort on the tot-adj-gifts field. Be sure to include the entire set of columns and rows in the range. Otherwise only part of the data table will be sorted, the scenarios will not follow the totals, and the spreadsheet will be a grand mess! Analysts should always save a copy of the spreadsheet before sorting as a backup, in case the sort does not come out as expected.

Table 6.2 is a sample of the results of a sort operation. Note that the total-costs column may have values that go beyond the current year's budget, or base-case level. The optimal solution without regard to the total budget will be the very first line of that column. In the example shown in Table 6.2, a total expenditure of $485,000 will provide an estimated $2,139,500 in gift revenue (tot adj gifts) in the coming year. However, to get a constrained optimal solution, the analyst looks to the line where the total allocation budget is equal to or less than the current base case of $245,000. The first line where this happens is line, or scenario number, 391, where $1,739,100 in net adjusted gifts is projected with $240,000 in total costs. This points to the constrained optimal solution. The analyst may want to look for the next higher level of funding and consider that scenario as well. For example, for $250,000 in total costs, a projected income of $1,761,500 represents an increase in net adjusted gifts raised of $22,400. A board might be convinced to increase funding by $5,000 to attempt to achieve this projected result.

The results from the sort operation should be recorded as shown in Tables 6.3, 6.4, and 6.5 for use in the next step in the process, which is translating the optimal solution into a budget plan for the coming year.

Table 6.2. Four Category-Funding Scenarios Sorted.[a]
(In thousands of dollars)

	Highest Funding Level	Slight Increase (Plus $5K from base)	Base Case	Constrained Optimal Solution	Lowest Funding Level
Scenario number	625	416	313	391	1
DM costs	150	120	100	120	50
DM gifts	808	650	500	650	240
PH costs	85	20	30	10	10
PH gifts	150	50	60	20	20
PI costs	150	90	65	90	20
PI gifts	1,000	900	700	900	100
PN costs	100	20	50	20	20
PN gifts	550	300	400	300	300
DM adj mult	1.05	1.05	1.05	1.05	1.05
DM adj gifts	690	562.5	425	562.5	202
PH adj mult	1.08	1.08	1.08	1.08	1.08
PH adj gifts	77	34	34.8	11.6	11.6
PI adj mult	1.1	1.1	1.1	1.1	1.1
PI adj gifts	950	900	705	900	90
PN adj mult	.95	.95	.95	.95	.95
PN adj gifts	422.5	265	330	265	265
Total costs	485	250	245	240	100
Tot adj gifts	2,139.5	1,761.5	1,494.8	1,739.1	568.6

[a]Change row headings to column headings and column headings to row headings when setting up the spreadsheet.

Table 6.3. Unbounded Optimal Solution.
(In dollars)

Category	Funding Level	Base-Case Funding Level	Difference Between Base and Funding Level
Direct mail	150,000	100,000	+50,000
Phone-a-thon	85,000	30,000	+55,000
Personal-individual	150,000	65,000	+85,000
Personal-nonindividual	100,000	50,000	+50,000
Total costs	485,000	245,000	+240,000

Table 6.4. Constrained Optimal Solution.
(In dollars)

Category	Funding Level	Base-Case Funding Level	Difference Between Base and Funding Level
Direct mail	120,000	100,000	+20,000
Phone-a-thon	10,000	30,000	−20,000
Personal-individual	90,000	65,000	+25,000
Personal-nonindividual	20,000	50,000	−30,000
Total costs	240,000	245,000	−5,000

Table 6.5. Slight-Increase Optimal Solution.
(In dollars)

Category	Funding Level	Base-Case Funding Level	Difference Between Base and Funding Level
Direct mail	120,000	100,000	+20,000
Phone-a-thon	20,000	30,000	−10,000
Personal-individual	90,000	65,000	+25,000
Personal-nonindividual	20,000	50,000	−30,000
Total costs	250,000	245,000	+5,000

How do these optimal solutions compare to using a direct cost-per-dollar-raised approach? In Table 5.1, the base case for each of the four categories was given as shown in Table 6.6, which also shows the cost per dollar raised.

Table 6.6. Base-Case Funding Levels.
(In dollars)

Category	Base-Case Funding	Gift Income	Cost Per Dollar
Direct mail	100,000	500,000	.20
Phone-a-thon	30,000	60,000	.50
Personal-individual	65,000	700,000	.09
Personal-nonindividual	50,000	400,000	.13

Using a cost-per-dollar ranking, funding should be moved away from the phone-a-thon and direct-mail programs and moved toward the more cost-efficient personal-individual and personal-nonindividual categories. Suppose the phone-a-thon funding is moved down two levels to $10,000 and the direct-mail funding is moved down one level to $90,000. Then funding to the personal-individual category is increased by two levels to $150,000 and the personal-nonindividual category is increased one level to $80,000. These increases and decreases are in relationship to the relative cost-per-dollar levels. More dollars are allocated to the more efficient categories.

The total funding level would then be $330,000 and the projected total adjusted gifts would be $1,753,500. This is only $14,400 more than the constrained optimal solution where the total costs were only $240,000. Spending $245,000 using the slight-increase optimal solution provides net gifts actually higher than the $330,000 cost level using the cost-per-dollar technique. Clearly, in principle, optimizing techniques can be dramatically superior to cost-per-dollar comparisons. How well optimizing works in reality is a function of how well the relationship between costs and gifts can be estimated for each category, and how well the organization can execute the action plan.

Sophisticated Model Approach

In large organizations, where the number of categories exceeds five and there are complexities such as crossover and carry-over effects that play an important role in the institution's fund-raising programs, some level of consulting services (whether internal programming support or external consulting services) will be required. At the minimum, the optimization process will require software that can handle a large number of categories and models described mathematically. If these minimal services are used, the analyst needs to prepare a list of parameters for the optimization process. The numbers consist of values for the parameters (a, b, c, d, g) indicated in Chapter Five, along with a description of the carryover and crossover effects that must be handled.

Consultants can provide results not only for the coming year but also for future years (typically three years out). In this way, the crossover and carryover effects will be accounted for and optimal solutions can be found for each year. However, it will still be up to the development office to decide which time period to use when selecting the best strategy. A solution that projects large increases in a ten-year period is not very useful to a nonprofit that seeks results in a shorter time frame, even if the ten-year projections are considerably higher than the short-term totals projected out to ten years.

Beyond using minimal consultation services, a development officer can also hire a firm to provide the historical analysis or to lead the entire Delphi process. However, for most non-profits, the costs of these more extensive services may be prohibitive. Furthermore, there is a benefit to the do-it-yourself approach. The more the development staff is involved, the better they will understand the process and the better they will trust the results.

Optimization at Northwestern University

In the Northwestern University study, ZS Associates provided the optimization software, which was developed by Zoltners and Sinha (1980). A formal description of the technique can be found in the literature cited earlier. The parameters associated with the functions described in Chapter Five provided the needed inputs for the optimization process. Given the models for each allocation category, optimal solutions were found.

Different levels of value-added multipliers were considered. Only one level ($1.50 per $1.00 in gifts for the highest priority category) is reported here. The process assumed that the total gift income level and the category allocation levels from fiscal year 1987–88 would be a reasonable base case for 1990–91. An unbounded case where there was no limit on the resource dollars was also analyzed to answer the question: If unlimited resources could be applied to the fund-raising effort, where should resources be best allocated?

The optimization point was confirmed by testing several data points around the optimal point using a decision support system set up with Lotus 123. This double check provided an assurance that the problem was set up correctly with the optimization software. This optimal solution represented the resource allocation levels that would project to a maximum benefit to the institution over the coming fiscal year (1990–91).

Unbounded Resources Optimization

Although it is unrealistic to expect a total development budget to be modified extensively to achieve optimal levels — the budget must be considered in relation to budgeting in other areas of the institution — the unbounded optimization case was considered for one of the Northwestern University scenarios. (A full description can be found in Lindahl, 1990, p. 107.) An unrestricted multiplier ($1.50) was used for the unbounded case because the results were, in some sense (total sum of the square of the difference from base case), the closest to the base case and hence the most conservative position. The optimal gift income (to the nearest million) was determined by examining many cases over a reasonable interval. The results (Table 6.7) show how the allocation changes as total resources are increased to the optimal levels.

The far left column of Table 6.7 represents how resources ($2.5 million) are allocated optimally (base case) for a total gift income of $58,206,000. As you increase the total resource level and move to the right in the table, eventually you get to the $13 million column. Any dollars allocated beyond $13 million

Table 6.7. Northwestern University Unbounded Optimal Solution.
(Unrestricted $1.50 multiplier, figures in thousands of dollars)

Category (Market-Technique-Type)	Funding 2.5M Dollars (Base)	Projected Gift Income from Six Levels of Funding (Base to Optimal)				Funding 13M Total Dollars (Optimal)
		Funding 3M Total Dollars	Funding 5M Total Dollars	Funding 7M Total Dollars	Funding 10M Total Dollars	
APA	0	0	50	210	500	845
APM	984	1,125	1,400	1,785	2,450	2,990
API	461	540	725	980	1,450	1,950
APB	87	105	175	280	550	910
AHA	0	0	200	350	600	780
ADA	0	195	850	1,015	1,200	1,365
PPA	0	0	0	0	0	0
PPM	25	30	50	70	100	130
PDA	12	15	25	35	50	65
NPA	12	15	25	35	100	130
NPM	0	0	400	980	1,400	1,755
NPI	75	90	125	175	300	455
NPB	12	15	25	35	100	195
CPM	361	375	400	455	500	585
FPM	461	495	550	595	700	845
Total adj net gifts	58,206	60,135	70,149	76,145	80,085	81,204

would cause the gift level to move below the $81,204,000 net gift amount for the $13 million column. Therefore, $13 million is the unbounded optimal level for Northwestern. The allocations in that column represent the needed funding levels for each category to raise the projected $81,204.000.

Notice that certain categories, such as nonindividual-personal-major (NPM), start at a $0 funding level and, as more money is available, the funding increases to some very high levels. Other categories, such as foundation-personal-major (FPM), start high and move to only a moderate funding level in the final unbounded optimal case (the far right column). Decision makers using only their intuition tend to follow a more linear pattern than this solution follows. Therefore, the absolute level of funding should matter when allocating fund-raising resources.

Base-Case Optimization

At Northwestern University the model was also constrained to the total-effort level of 1987–88 ($2,490,470). This result (with modifications reviewed in Chapter Seven) was the one used in the strategic planning process. The results that were calculated using the optimization software are shown in Table 6.8.

The table shows a projected difference in adjusted gift income from $63,708,575 (base case) to $80,071,107 (optimal case). This projected adjusted increase of $16,362,532 holds the effort level fixed at $2,490,470. Several categories have an allocation level of $0; however, in practice, a category cannot be

Table 6.8. Northwestern University Constrained Optimization.
(Full $1.50 multiplier, figures in dollars)

Category (Market-Technique-Type)	Base Case		Optimal Case	
	Funding Level	Adjusted Net Gift Income	Funding Level	Adjusted Net Gift Income
APA	170,000	1,648,046	0	776,529
APM	538,220	11,245,818	1,045,998	17,905,840
API	155,090	5,004,254	460,737	9,249,959
APB	96,620	3,249,320	74,714	3,055,114
AHA	218,030	785,543	0	47,766
ADA	587,770	2,640,245	0	161,218
PPA	1,360	60,608	0	61,569
PPM	37,170	392,365	0	82,346
PDA	17,560	81,560	0	3,907
NPA	33,950	717,091	12,452	627,992
NPM	165,230	4,206,800	0	3,771,220
NPI	34,700	2,080,550	62,262	2,446,470
NPB	35,880	449,466	12,452	346,145
CPA (crossover from AHA)	N/A	620,084	N/A	131,500
CPA (crossover from ADA)	N/A	1,199,752	N/A	263,000
CPM	200,470	15,494,461	361,118	19,869,496
FPM	198,420	13,832,612	460,737	21,271,036
Totals	2,490,470	63,708,575	2,490,470	80,071,107

removed completely from funding in one year. In the next chapter, the process of converting the model optimization results into the fund-raising operation's actual strategic plan is reviewed. This conversion is a complex process that must take into account potential organizational problems that can arise from the changes.

Implementing
the Strategic Plan

The optimization process described in Chapter Six provides an allocation strategy that optimizes adjusted gift income for the period of time chosen by the steering committee. The next task is to convert these raw-dollar recommendations into a meaningful and workable fund-raising budget, or strategy.

As the fund-raising strategy is set, descriptions of the programs represented by each category and the program's particular implementation plans should also be formalized. Fund-raising staff need to see this strategic plan and understand the overall rationale behind cuts to some budgets and increases to other budgets. The board of directors should also share in the final planning document in order to understand where all the resources are going and how they will be spent.

Creating a Plan

Converting the resource allocation numbers into a real plan can be difficult. There may be constraints that were not (but in some cases should have been) a part of the analytical model — for example, minimum funding levels, personnel issues, or the financial health of the entire organization. Change also carries with it costs that may not have been appropriately incorporated into the model.

For example, a large computerized phone system may have been purchased two years ago for the organization's phone-a-thon program. This system now provides on-line interactive calling in which the prospects' phone numbers are automatically dialed and connected to the callers. The original estimate for the potential success of the automated-calling project showed gross gains of an extra $300,000 per year for the organization's annual fund. The cost of the new equipment spread out over three years was $400,000, so that the net increase in gifts was to be around $500,000 over three years.

The resource allocation plan, however, may show that the phone-a-thon program needs to be cut back extensively when compared to the potential gains for the same resource dollars in other fund-raising programs. Converting the optimization numbers into a strategic plan in this case may mean that the phone-a-thon program has to stay funded at the level determined earlier, in order to at least break even on the capital investment in equipment. If the steering committee had thought these kinds of issues through ahead of time, minimum-funding levels for particular programs could have been built into the model itself. Also, if an organization chooses to use the simpler of the two optimization techniques, the fact that only the five funding scenarios predetermined in the Delphi process are used should help to prevent nonimplementable solutions or strategies, since those five will be the only funding levels used in the optimization process.

Personnel issues may also prevent the optimal allocation of resources. For example, an organization might have recently hired three additional major-gift fund-raising professionals. None of the three has experience or training in planned giving (bequests and irrevocable trusts); however, the allocation recommendation calls for a large increase in resources for the planned-giving program. The one officer currently employed in planned giving should, in theory, be upgraded to a staff of two, and the major-gift area should be reduced by one staff member. Training for the person to be added to the planned-giving staff might take anywhere from six months to a year and might incur costs for sending the person to training conferences. In this instance, allocations may have to be adjusted over a two- or three-year period.

Finally, consider an organization that is in financial trouble, lacking in endowment funds, and dependent on tuition or other programmatic revenue sources. Suppose the optimal resource allocation shows that a shift to long-term programs such as planned giving and major gifts is preferable to remaining with short-term programs such as direct mail and phone-a-thons. The process may have been set up to consider optimization over a three-year time frame. In this instance, the organization might have to move slowly over several years to the new allocation levels. Otherwise, the lack of current-use dollars during the coming year may cause the organization to go out of business before the long-term dollars begin to come in.

The strategic planning steering committee needs to review the discussions from the two-day Delphi process concerning funding levels. A tape recording of these discussions about how to implement increases and decreases in funding for programs provides a place to start developing the strategic plan. After listening to the give and take for each category, the committee should note the differences in implementation that would become possible at the resource allocation level suggested by the optimization process. Continuing the example from Chapter Six, consider the simple resource allocation shown in Table 7.1.

Table 7.1. Optimal Allocation of Differences from Base.
(In dollars)

Category	Base Case	Optimal Allocation	Difference
Direct mail	100,000	120,000	+20,000
Phone-a-thon	30,000	10,000	−20,000
Personal-individual	65,000	90,000	+25,000
Personal-nonindividual	50,000	20,000	−30,000
Total costs	245,000	240,000	−5,000
Total gifts	1,660,000	1,739,100	+79,100

For each category, a definitive plan needs to be determined for implementing the new allocation level. During the Delphi process, many different options will have been discussed. For some categories, there may have been a particular option that the respondents agreed would be best. In that event, the steering committee can work to fine tune that option. However, the Delphi respondents may not have agreed on how to spend the additional (or fewer) dollars. Here, the committee needs both to review the suggestions from the Delphi process and to consider other alternatives.

For example, the committee might consider increasing the direct-mail budget by $20,000: How would this actually be done? In the Delphi process, the following suggestions might have been made: (1) purchase additional lists and send out two additional mailings per year to these exploratory markets, (2) increase the quality of the pieces already going out by doing the mail/merge on laser printers instead of using pressure-sensitive labels for two of the mailings, (3) hire an additional person (a part-time consultant) who has extensive creative skills and can produce better-looking pieces, or (4) increase the number of mailings to the same audience this year. If the Delphi participants agreed that option two was the most reasonable, that would become the basis for the implementation of the new resource level. Alternatively, if the Delphi participants could not agree on an option, the steering committee would explore all four options along with new suggestions. In consultation with the head of the direct-mail program, the best option would be determined.

In addition, the committee might think about taking $20,000 away from the phone-a-thon budget. First of all, recall that in this example (Tables 6.3, 6.4, 6.5, and 7.1) no *optimal* allocation strategy appears that is exactly at the base-case level of total funding ($245,000). Although this would not occur using the more sophisticated optimization techniques, it can happen when considering only five funding levels for each category. Looking to the next higher level of funding ($250,000) (Table 6.5), we can see that the only difference is a $10,000 increase in the phone-a-thon funding level. It would probably be safe to interpret this as implying that we may not need to eliminate a full $20,000 from the funding, but rather $15,000. Several different ideas for cutting the funding level may have developed within the Delphi process: (1) call the same group of people less often (once instead of twice a year), (2) change to volunteer callers, instead of paid callers, (3) reduce the size of the population to be called by limiting this year's calls to past donors or to recent donors, (4) reduce the size of the population to be called by using an outside service to rank prospects using geodemographics or other systems. (However, this may cost too much if the service is hired exclusively for this one program.) Once again the committee may need to come up with other plans, either because the Delphi participants could not agree on an option, or the option they supported may not fit into the overall strategy. The head of the particular program being discussed should also be a part of this debate.

The committee might determine that the optimal $25,000 increase in resources for the personal solicitation of individuals for major gifts could be implemented in these ways: (1) add a junior-level development officer to make many cold calls by allocating part of the corporate-foundation officers time (the current major-gift person could follow up with prospects as needed after the cold calls are made by the reallocated officers), (2) produce a better-looking annual report or other stewardship piece to encourage further giving of large gifts, (3) replace the current major-gift officer (through attrition) with someone who has more experience with planned giving as well as major gifts (and offer a higher salary for the position). Suppose option three was agreed to by the Delphi participants. The steering committee would then use this option as a base, perhaps making adjustments to it in order to fit it into the overall development operation plan.

Handling the decrease of funding ($30,000) for corporate and foundation fund raising would be the most difficult task. Certainly the one fund raiser in this area would have to be at least partially reallocated to another area (to personal solicitation of individuals—mentioned above in number 1). There is no other solution when such large dollars are taken away from a program.

Using Cutback Strategies

The previous discussion illustrates that a new allocation strategy will naturally involve the cutback of fund-raising dollars to certain programs. During the recessionary times of the early 1990s, the issue of how to cut back is one that is important to most nonprofits. Practically the entire September 1991 issue of *CASE Currents* (Taylor, 1991) was dedicated to the topic of how campus fund raisers, alumni officers, and communicators are coping with budget cuts. Any steering committee looking for creative ways to implement a reduction in a particular program should look through this issue for ideas that can be applied in the determination of a nonprofit's fund-raising strategy.

Another important reference regarding ways to reduce funding levels is "Predictive Models for Annual Fund and Major Gift Fund Raising" (Lindahl and Winship, 1991). The paper considers how to identify the prospects who are most likely to give gifts at two different levels: major ($100,000+ over three years) and annual ($1,000+ over three years). The model for the higher level helps identify prospects whom an organization should visit personally, and it provides the focus to consolidate resources on the best potential prospects. The model consists of internal data such as age and past giving, and externally provided data such as geodemographic census information available from special services or consultants. The model for the lower-level prospects uses the same variables as the base and adds in several other factors, such as whether the spouse is also an alumnus and whether the prospect holds a high business position.

The annual-fund model is being used at Northwestern to eliminate prospects most unlikely to give a gift over $1,000 in a three-year period. A 140,000-record mailing list was cut back to around 100,000 records with very little difference in results. To prevent elimination of the most recent alumni and the reunion-year alumni (two important prospect groups for universities), these groups were hard-coded into the selection criteria for the mailing list.

The major-gift model predictor score, known at Northwestern as the Lindahl/Winship number, is now printed out on the bottom of every Northwestern prospect-tracking summary report or prospect card. The number serves as an additional indicator to help put into perspective the information listed as individual characteristics.

In both of the models, it is not surprising that past giving is the strongest single factor in predicting who will give in the future (although considering all the data in the models is a superior predictor overall). Recency of giving is also important. These two factors have been traditionally used in fund raising, with labels such as LYBUNTS (last year but unfortunately not this year), PYBUNTS (past years but unfortunately not this year), and NEVER GIVERS. This research puts these factors on a statistically sound footing and provides a way to weight characteristics not related to giving (salary level, affluence, age) and past giving when determining whom to ask for a gift.

If practitioners have been using segmentation based on past giving for years, why is the power of statistics needed? Why not just use an ad hoc or intuitive approach to market segmentation? The argument for statistical analyses is that they allow development officers to utilize a considerable amount of information simultaneously. They can use not only their own experiences but also those of others both within their own and in other institutions.

The findings I have been discussing are in contrast to the more recent work done to compare prospects for major outright gifts and irrevocable trusts (Lindahl, 1991). I reported the discovery that outright past giving was statistically significant only for outright major-gift prospects and not for irrevocable-trust prospects. The key factors for donors of irrevocable trusts were past irrevocable-trust gifts and the age of the prospect. Other variables, described in Lindahl (1991), were significant as well. Using these results, the development office could concentrate irrevocable-trust development effort in a reduced population of irrevocable-gift prospects, improving the efficiency of the fund-raising process.

Creating a Final Planning Document

Whether or not these statistical models are used in the effort to cut back on the resources allocated to the annual-fund, major-gift, or planned-giving programs, the steering committee will need to create a document that provides suggestions for adjusting each program's funding levels. The committee then looks for implementation difficulties among the suggestions, such as conflicts between programs. It may be that two programs may want to increase the number of evenings they give to phone-a-thon work, but the equipment is already in use each evening. From this list, a single strategy for each category is identified as the most feasible. These are compiled into another document that takes the single strategy for each category and expands it into a plan that shows exactly where the money should be spent.

For example, the suggestion that a direct-mail program increase the quality of each mailing piece by using mail/merge laser printing would be expanded to provide cost estimates from different vendors, budget line changes demanded by the plan (even if these changes are outside of the particular program's budget lines), samples of the quality of output desired, and a description of the research showing other nonprofits' success using this technology. The head of each program could be asked to provide such an expansion of the single suggested strategy.

All the expanded strategies are put together in a final document, which includes a combined line-item budget that describes where particular funds need to be increased or decreased. This final plan provides the blueprint for action that represents the third phase in the overall strategic planning process. This plan should be circulated to the entire development staff, board, and other key staff members in the organization. Each development officer should clearly see the role being played by the other programs and should understand the expected goals to be achieved within his or her own program.

The planning document can also be expanded to include some or all of the following items:

- An introduction to the strategic planning process
- Definitions and descriptions of categories
- The mission statement and descriptions of constraints and priority multipliers
- Optimal allocation levels

- The implementation strategy, including the expanded description of the plan for each category and the budget line-item changes
- The multiyear direction for each category
- The goals for each category

The next section describes the strategy based on optimization analysis that was recommended for Northwestern University.

Northwestern University Allocation Recommendations

The results of the constrained optimization routine for Northwestern University (Table 6.8) showed a clear trend away from APA (alumni-personal-annual), NPM (nonalumni-personal-major), and ADA (alumni–direct mail–annual) and toward APM (alumni-personal-major), FPM (foundation-personal-major), API (alumni-personal-irrevocable), CPM (corporate-personal-major), APB (alumni-personal-bequest), NPI (non-alumni-personal-irrevocable), and NPB (nonalumni-personal-bequest). More emphasis needed to be placed on the long-term categories, especially major-gifts from corporations, foundations, and alumni and irrevocable gifts from alumni and nonalumni.

Based on these results, my specific allocation recommendations for Northwestern University included five items:

1.   If possible, increase the total allocation of development resources by $2 million to $3 million.
2.   Add two persons each to corporate and foundation fund raising. One person in each pair should be on the development staff at the appropriate school (one corporate officer at the graduate school of management and one foundation officer at the medical school), and the other person at the central development office.
3.   If the total resource level cannot be increased, trim back the direct-mail and phone-a-thon programs by concentrating on the most productive markets — those with the highest potential and interest. Reallocate staff as appropriate.
4.   Add two additional major-gift fund raisers in the solicitation of irrevocable gifts from alumni.

5. Reallocate the time of development officers working with individuals away from soliciting nonalumni major and annual gifts and alumni annual gifts and toward soliciting alumni major and irrevocable gifts.

As the full optimization models have shown (Table 6.7), Northwestern's development operation is underfunded. A conservative projection was that increasing the resource dollars by $2 million to $3 million per year and allocating those dollars appropriately would account for increases in new gift dollars somewhere in the neighborhood of $10 million to $20 million (net) per year.

As described earlier in this chapter, the final strategic plan is usually a modified version of the allocation levels from the model. Modifications in the strategic plan at Northwestern University were made by the vice president of development, the development executive committee, and the central budget administration.

Because of the experimental nature of this process at Northwestern University, the recommendations carried less weight in the final budget-making process than would normally be the case. (In other situations, the more involved the head of the fund-raising operation or the chief budget officer becomes in the planning process, the more the recommendations will be integrated into the final budget statements.)

Therefore, at Northwestern, the first recommendation, to increase resources at the $2 million to $3 million level, was not approved by the central administration. Instead, resources were increased by $447,000, or 18 percent of the base case (the 1987–88 level).

The corporate and foundation fund-raising areas were going through personnel changes during the years of the study. From 1986 to the late 1980s the actual number of development officers employed went from six to two. Although two additional persons were not added as my second recommendation suggested, the number of officers for the nonindividual markets was restored to four. The vice president's concern over the soft economy was the major reason for not fully implementing this recommendation. This environmental factor could have been incorporated into the optimization process, but was not in this case.

Although not implemented until the start of fiscal 1991–92, my third recommendation resulted in a massive trim back of 40,000 alumni prospects (out of 140,000) and a greatly reduced cost for the phone-a-thon and direct-mail programs. A statistical model was used to determine which annual-fund prospects to eliminate.

With the recent (1987) creation of a planned and major gift department—and the increase in the number of development officers—there was some concern about increasing the level of effort in this area even further. The major gifts raised by this group are long-term income. Even so, resources to this area were increased by $156,000, a 101 percent increase, approximately equal to my fourth recommendation.

The overriding considerations for modifying my fifth recommendation, to reallocate officers' time, were similar to the concerns about the fourth recommendation. The alumni-personal-major and alumni-personal-irrevocable categories were increased by $107,000 and $156,000, respectively. However, the nonalumni categories were increased instead of decreased as the recommendation called for, because the medical school allocated resources not under control by central development to increase resources dedicated to its nonalumni market (grateful patients). This demonstrates the problem that may come from lack of central budget control in a large organization. What may seem to one unit or region as an appropriate area in which to increase funding may not appear appropriate from a central perspective.

The results of these modifications were then incorporated into a final budget document for the Office of Development and Alumni Relations at Northwestern University.

8

Monitoring Results
and Making Corrections

The blueprint for action described in Chapter Seven, which is
distributed to all involved personnel, contains a review of the
mission of the fund-raising department, a detailed description
of the strategy for resource allocation for the various program
categories, a line-by-line budget that shows how the entire operation will be funded over the coming year, and a set of goals
for each program to achieve. Once the blueprint for action is
implemented, there remains the task of monitoring the progress
of goal achievement. In the words of Lorange (1980), we must
now consider, in detail, "Control — How do we know if we are
on track?" The key to this control is to accurately report the
progress of fund-raising efforts and to regularly adjust the strategy throughout the year in response to unforeseen factors that
arise from both internal and external forces.

The first of these key issues — accurately reporting fund-
raising progress — was addressed in Chapter Three in the dis-

cussion of historical analysis. Organizations that have completed a historical analysis have simultaneously laid the groundwork for an effective feedback mechanism. The progress report must take into account the multiyear payout of pledges, the extremely long delay in receipt of bequests from the time the bequest expectancy is recorded, and the current value of irrevocable trusts that are normally recorded at their full market value. These three requirements are accomplished by converting the pledges, bequests, and trusts into their current-year value. The report, produced on a monthly basis, should divide the gifts into the same programs or categories that were used in the historical analysis. Remember that the multipliers used in the optimization process to ensure that priority categories received higher resource allocations should now be either removed completely from both the goals and the year-to-date gifts or used in adjusting both figures. Table 8.1 shows how such a report might look.

Table 8.1. Year-to-Date Fund-Raising Progress Toward Goals.
(In dollars)

Category	Year-to-Date Adjusted Gifts	Year-to-Date Goals	Difference	Difference (percent)
Direct mail	500,000	650,000	−150,000	−23
Phone-a-thon	25,000	20,000	5,000	25
Personal-individual	800,000	900,000	−100,000	−11
Personal-nonindividual	350,000	300,000	50,000	17

A final version of this report would be presented as a part of the Delphi process for the following year. Other reports should be produced monthly to show how the year-to-date totals compared to the predicted totals for the proportion of the year already completed. To be even more accurate, last year's results could be used to divide the goal into sums that reflect the proportion of gifts usually received at certain times of the year. For example, December and January are usually very strong fundraising months for nonprofits. Therefore, the goals associated with these months could be set higher than one-twelfth of the total goal.

How should an organization respond to the year-to-date reports? On a monthly basis, the reports should serve to reinforce success in a particular program as well as to challenge those areas where the results are less than the projected goal at that time. This will differ from what is usually done in nonprofits, because these projected goals were built with the relationship between resources and results specifically in mind. If a program's goals were raised, it was either because additional resources were dedicated to that particular program or because the responsiveness of the program's market to fund-raising effort was estimated to have changed.

In addition, the use of an adjusted report prevents the problem of recently hired personnel taking credit for gifts that were raised by the effort of staff from two or three years ago. It also prevents newly hired staff being blamed for a decrease in the level of gifts in the current year when the lack of effort of earlier staff might be to blame. The large amount of turnover in development staff further exacerbates these two problems (55 percent of higher education fund raisers are in their first or second year in their positions, Carbone, 1987). The possibility of not receiving credit for their work can cause insecurity among development officers, subtly influencing them to ask for and accept lower dollar level gifts from prospects at the end of the year, instead of working toward long-range cultivation of potential high-level donors.

On a yearly basis, the reports serve an additional function as well, that of providing feedback on the accuracy of the model itself. Certain programs may have followed the exact specifications of the strategic plan spelled out in the blueprint for action. For example, in Table 8.1, the sample direct-mail program shows a $150,000 shortfall against the goal at the end of the year. This represents a 23 percent decrease over what was expected. Now the staff must consider why the program did not reach goal. If the implementation of the strategy came off without problem, the underlying estimate of the relationship between resources and results could be at fault. The current year's results become a part of the historical analysis for the next year so that the planning session participants can judge if the relationship itself needs to be adjusted.

It is also essential to remember that situations change from year to year. Recently, the public's perception of the financial responsibility of several universities has swung like a pendulum from positive to negative. For example, Stanford University is "struggling to recover from a damaging financial scandal." Stanford's president, Donald Kennedy, "announced his resignation [in the summer of 1991] amid allegations that Stanford had overbilled the federal government millions of dollars for research expenses, including bills for flowers and furniture for Kennedy's house" (Lev, 1992, p. 11). Whether or not this news will affect the fund-raising effort at Stanford is yet to be seen and difficult to predict. However, the event does demonstrate how quickly an organization's public image can change.

Nonprofit television and radio preaching ministries have seen gifts shrink as the public image of their organizations has shifted. For example, the PTL ministries collapsed under a scandal surrounding the founding leader. More recently, the resignation of the president of the national United Way over allegations of fund misuse is of concern to that organization's fund raisers.

These occurrences demonstrate that the relationship between resources and funds raised is not a constant but will need to be adjusted as circumstances change. How do development officers make these changes and incorporate them into their strategic plans for the coming year? As the development staff goes through the Delphi process, the issues affecting particular programs will be discussed, and the participants will estimate results based on their new understanding of the organization in relation to the various markets. These new estimates can then be incorporated into a new model for the coming year, with the optimization process guiding the way to a fresh and creative blueprint for action for the next year(s).

Even if the final results are way off the goals, the organization should not give up on the planning process and revert back to the intuitive approach to fund-raising management. The optimization process is only as good as the estimates it uses, and an organization just starting to use the process may not yet be very good at estimating. Moreover, research through the past twenty years has shown a direct relationship between effort and results in nonprofit fund raising (Leslie, 1969; Pickett, 1977; Leslie and Ramey, 1985; Loessin, 1987). For example, Loessin found that for all institutional types in higher education, total voluntary support was highly correlated (over .70) with fundraising expenditures. Estimating the relationship precisely for a particular program is not easy, but theory and research back the task as a worthwhile one.

Although nonprofit use of the strategic planning process described in this book is currently limited to Northwestern University, hundreds of corporations have used these concepts for over ten years to help allocate their sales forces. The concepts have a strong track record in for-profit organizations, and there is reason to believe that these positive results are attainable by nonprofits as well.

Davey L. Willans, director of field force development, international operations, for Warner-Lambert Company, a pharmaceutical firm based in Morris Plains, New Jersey, has worked with a consulting company specializing in sales force allocation for close to ten years and has utilized their services in some twenty-three different countries. Willans says his experience provides support for using a strategic planning process.

> One of the best ways for any organization to grow is to allocate [its] resources in the most optimal way. This may seem obvious, as deciding how to utilize currently available resources is a job managers do every day. Unfortunately, resource allocation decisions are often based upon pre-conceived ideas or limited and/or somewhat prejudiced historical experience of the manager.
>
> Most major companies in the pharmaceutical industry have very extensive product lines and have to make decisions about which products will receive marketing support. In our industry, the field sales representatives are the most productive promotional resource available, yet, they are also the most costly. It is, therefore, imperative that, when

planning how to use this resource, the decision should not be limited to just one or two managers that may have self-serving interests. The "Field Force Strategy Study Process" . . . has helped overcome these problems. Since 1983 this process has proven to be very beneficial in helping management in 23 different countries, to address very basic questions of field force resource allocation [personal communication with author, 1991].

Many companies using this kind of strategic planning process have found that in addition to assisting management teams in identifying an optimal field force strategy, the process yields these additional benefits:

- Enhanced appreciation and understanding on the part of the entire management team as to how the field force resources should be allocated
- Higher commitment to the plan that is developed
- Improved communication between different managerial disciplines
- Improved management ability to reassess decisions as changes in the marketplace occur
- More objective and consistent evaluations of the Field Force resource

Not all of these benefits will transfer to nonprofit organizations' use of these techniques in the fund-raising strategy process, but certainly the validity of the basic process has been confirmed over and over again in the for-profit sales environment.

Northwestern University Results

The results for the fiscal year 1990–91 are now in for Northwestern University. Although we have not yet gone through a second year of the Delphi process, Table 8.2 has been developed to show the differences between expected and actual results for the sixteen categories that were considered in the process.

(These gift numbers have been adjusted using the multipliers described earlier, which give more value to those categories closer to the mission of Northwestern's development operation.) For example, in the second row, APM (alumni-personal-major) shows a base case of 538, meaning that $538,000 was allocated to this category in 1987–88. The next column shows that $645,000 was allocated in fiscal 1990–91 to personally raise major gifts from alumni. The right three columns show the gifts that were predicted using the model ($13,629,000), the actual gifts (pledges, irrevocable trusts, and bequests adjusted as described earlier) ($13,247,000), and the difference between the two ($382,000), 2.8 percent less than predicted.

Some categories show larger differences between the goals and the results. Northwestern will need to consider those and either work to increase the effort, to motivate staff, or to re-adjust the response curves to reflect a change in market responsiveness. Although Northwestern has not gone through this process yet, the following discussion demonstrates some of the issues that might be raised.

The categories API (alumni-personal-irrevocable) and NPI (nonalumni-personal-irrevocable) both had predicted values much higher than the actual amounts received. One reason for the difference might be the change in the tax laws after 1986. In addition, looking back three or four years at the gifts coming into these categories, there are several years where the level of gifts was, in retrospect, abnormally high. These unusual years caused the Delphi respondents to predict a greater annual response to effort than was realistic. The model for these categories should be adjusted to reflect the more recent past.

The AHA (alumni–phone-a-thon–annual) and ADA (alumni–direct mail–annual) categories' results were higher than predicted. Two years before (1988–89 and 1989–90), Northwestern was in the final phase of its Campaign for Great Teachers, which involved a special direct-mail and phone-a-thon appeal to all College of Arts and Sciences alumni. Some effort recorded in these years may have resulted in additional gifts for fiscal 1990–91. On the other hand, the higher results may just reflect superior staff performance in these categories, or

Table 8.2. Northwestern University Comparison of Predicted and Actual Gifts.
(In thousands of dollars)

Category (market-technique-type)	Allocations		Gifts			
	1987–88 Base Case	1990–91 Actual	1990–91 Predicted	1990–91 Actual	Difference	Difference (percent)
APA	170	237	2,104	2,230	126	5.99
APM	538	645	13,629	13,247	-382	-2.80
API	155	311	7,895	1,222	-6,673	-84.52
APB	97	180	3,928	2,126	-1,802	-45.88
AHA	218	208	962	1,146	184	19.13
ADA	588	597	3,300	3,792	492	14.91
PPA	1	0	61	94	33	54.10
PPM	37	17	234	683	449	191.88
PDA	18	12	85	80	-5	-5.88
NPA	34	34	751	1,079	328	43.68
NPM	165	226	4,764	1,621	-3,143	-65.97
NPI	35	66	2,549	423	-2,126	-83.41
NPB	36	76	610	1,112	502	82.30
CPA			1,828	2,038	210	11.49
CPM	200	176	14,203	14,867	664	4.68
FPM	198	152	11,293	9,907	-1,386	-12.27
Totals	2,490	2,937	68,196	55,667	-12,529	-18.37

perhaps they reflect the net increase in the number of alumni available for solicitation (4,000 new alumni are added each year to the pool).

The resources allocated to the NPM (nonalumni-personal-major) category were almost doubled from the base case ($165,000 increased to $226,000). The gifts received, however, were way down from what was projected to come in. Since most of the increase in effort occurred during 1990–91, results from this category may take a year or two to reflect the increase in effort. In fact, a gift of $10,000,000 Northwestern recently received from a nonalumnus (given in fiscal 1991–92) will do just that!

The results in the nonindividual categories CPM (corporate-personal-major) and FPM (foundation-personal-major) are each slightly off from predicted levels. The corporate results are 5 percent greater than predicted — an acceptable level of difference. The foundation category received around 12 percent less than predicted. This might reflect the fact that the foundation program was cut back to around one FTE staff member a few years back. Recalling that the typical delays in response for this market are over a year also makes this level of difference more understandable.

Each of the other categories will be discussed at Northwestern as well, in order to suggest how particular circumstances could have affected the relationship between costs and results. Based on this analysis, either the model used for the next year will be adjusted or the staff will be motivated or further trained to provide for superior implementation of the fund-raising process.

Scientific Validation

In all of the earlier discussion concerning control issues, the focus was comparing actual results with estimated goals for each category and using this analysis as a basis for discussion of the coming year's estimates. However, this form of validation does not really address the issue of "scientific" validation of strategic planning results. What is needed for scientific validation is some type of control group, such as one of two identical nonprofits implementing strategy A (base case), while the other implements strategy B (optimal case). Obviously, this is impossible. The following discussion presents a different possible validation process that a development operation might want to consider.

Like any model of a complex interdependent system, the model proposed in this study is very difficult to validate beyond the simple comparison between actual and predicted dollars mentioned earlier. In the for-profit world, studies that model the analogous sales force allocation problem are rarely validated in a rigorous way. The cost is extensive and the time required prevents the results from being used in a timely fashion. The strategic planning models for Northwestern, for example, predicted the level of gift income (in current-year adjusted dollars) for fiscal year 1990–91. In order to begin the validation process, a good portion of the year would have had to have been concluded. Assuming that the validation would take a few months to complete, the results would only be available toward the end of the current year. This would not allow enough time to adjust the current year's allocation strategy. Furthermore, it takes time to implement an allocation change; staff must be retrained and programs reconfigured to a smaller or larger size. All these problems together can lead observers to confuse a slow beginning with a successful conclusion. Because of these difficulties, a model may not always be validated.

However, the following approach can assist development officers in articulating an ideal validation of the model. The approach involves conducting an experiment during the fiscal year and comparing results, and it also handles the problem of external influences in the fund-raising process. In this approach, the prospect pool is randomly split into two groups, A and B. Then, during the year, effort is given to each group with two different allocation strategies, SA and SB. SA takes the base case — divided by two — to simulate what would have happened with the control allocations. SB takes the optimal allocation strategy — divided by two — to simulate what would have happened with the experimental allocations. At the end of the fiscal year, the gift results from the two groups would be compared.

Even this approach has two problems. The first comes from the fact that some categories will be staffed at such low levels, or distributed in such small quantities across several staff, that the split will be difficult to manage. For instance, how can exactly one-half of a person's time be allocated to prospects in group A and one-eighth to the prospects in group B?

The second problem is central to other validation methods as well — the time frame is too short to reveal the true relationship between short-term programs such as direct mail and long-term programs such as personal solicitation of major gifts. Further study is needed regarding this relationship over a twenty- or thirty-year time frame.

Of the techniques mentioned, only the first (comparing actual and predicted gift income) will be practical on a year-by-year basis for a nonprofit. Comparing the expected and actual results, although not perfect, does provide an excellent basis for extensive discussion regarding how well programs were executed over the previous year and how markets are reacting differently to the nonprofit from year to year. Any resource allocation model will only be as good as the estimates on which it is based. Instead of employing a scientific method to check the accuracy of the model for a particular year, officers must validate the model through the reporting process and the ongoing feedback that occurs as the strategic fund-raising plans evolve over the history of the nonprofit.

Conclusion:
Strategic Issues
in Fund Raising

The methodology outlined in this book provides a framework to begin the strategic planning process for nonprofit fund-raising operations. Based on the four phases associated with Lorange's (1980) strategic planning systems — mission, strategies, budgets, and control — the process involves a directed combination of historical and judgmental data. Estimates from Delphi sessions balance a historical analysis of fund-raising efforts and their relationship to gift income. Without the judgmental input from the Delphi process, the organization cannot take into account the internal and external environmental changes that affect the fund-raising process.

Due to the combination of historical and judgmental techniques, unexpected large gifts can also be handled by the planning methodology. A historical analysis would show any unexpected large gift as an outlier. This could be taken into account, using the best judgment of the development staff, when setting up the predictive model.

The optimization process at the heart of the methodology is solidly based on the concept of comparing marginal increases in gifts, as opposed to comparing cost per dollar raised. Consideration of the results of the next dollars allocated to a category, or program, instead of the results of the current dollars, provides a way to optimally allocate fund-raising resources.

A steering committee organizes the actual strategic planning process. A historical analysis of the past few years' costs and results provides a base case for a consideration of the funding levels and projected gift income for the coming years. A Delphi session is scheduled for a two-day retreat with up to twenty staff members. Judgmental data is collected and discussions are recorded that consider how programs could be modified to reflect appropriate funding level increases or decreases. A model based on these data is then optimized to provide a resource allocation strategy. The committee converts this strategy into a budget blueprint for action, which is used to compare the coming year's actual results to predicted results. The process is repeated on a yearly basis, using the prior year's results as a starting point.

Benefits of Strategic Planning

Assuming this yearly strategic planning process is carried out correctly, it will enable the nonprofit to spend scarce fund-raising resources in the most efficient way possible (within the limits of the estimation process). In addition, there are other less easily quantifiable benefits. First, management will be better able to judge the performance of fund-raising staff, and management will also be able to set goals that are compatible with the level of resources allocated. Second, there will be a higher commitment to the plan by all staff members, because of their participation in the process. Third, a better understanding of the nonprofit's markets and programs will result. The staff members' level of understanding will build progressively during the years of the planning process as historical data is combined with the judgmental input of the development officers who meet the markets every day. Fourth, the key decision makers will be discussing the most important issues of the whole fund-raising operation — not just each particular decision maker's small area of interest.

The decision makers will be able to move from a short- to a long-term horizon and to ensure that the mission of the organization is considered in the planning process.

How to Get Started

The methodology can be implemented over a wide range of investment levels — anywhere from using in-house staff and an electronic spreadsheet to bringing in a consultant to compile the historical analysis, run the two-day Delphi session, and develop the optimal strategy using sophisticated software programs. The key is simply to begin somewhere along the continuum and start to take advantage of this new approach to planning at some level.

The typical first step for any organization is to begin to track gifts using the adjusted reporting concepts described earlier. Without knowing the current value of pledges, bequest expectancies, and irrevocable trusts, comparisons between different categories involving these gifts will not be useable. Moreover, producing this report of adjusted gift income will help development staff better understand the results of their efforts on a year-by-year basis.

A second step might be to begin monitoring costs. This might involve sending a survey, organized by fund-raising program, to all development staff. The questions the survey should ask include: Where are you spending your fund-raising dollars? How have you changed your allocation levels over the past several years? And, once costs are known: How do your costs relate to the gifts coming in?

Step three might be an experimental deployment of the strategic planning process. Development officers could begin getting into the cycle of defining a mission, setting strategies, working out budgets, and establishing methods of control. The electronic spreadsheet approach can be used to keep costs down; the number of allocation categories to be considered can be limited; the initial planning retreat can be restricted to a small group of participants; and the results of the retreat can be compared to the results of the current planning process. However, even in such an experimental process, the head of the development operation should be directly and closely involved.

The fourth step could involve repeating the process in the second year with additional allocation categories and greater staff participation. A programmer could be hired to convert the electronic spreadsheet optimization process to a standard computer program (a relatively easy task). This would allow more than five categories to be used in the model.

Finally, the fifth step might involve bringing in a consultant team to do an extensive historical analysis of the fund-raising operation and to run the Delphi sessions. The consulting firm should have some direct or analogous experience, such as working with sales force allocations.

Every nonprofit organization will be able to use the strategic planning process at some level. Remember that a long journey begins with the first step. Taking that step will not be without difficulty, but the potential rewards to the organization and to humanity will be worth the effort.

Northwestern University Study Results

In addition to providing the basis for the development of the methodology described in this book, the Northwestern University study also provided several general results and conclusions for nonprofits. Although these results may be more immediately meaningful to those interested in university development, others will be able to use the information to begin thinking about similar issues in other contexts. In addition, the results described here are mainly the major results—not every subproject result. Readers interested in the secondary results are referred to Lindahl (1990). Following a summary of major results and of three main considerations in the study (delay factors, priority levels, and crossover effects), I discuss how past fund-raising research relates to these findings.

Summary of Major Results

Long-Term Gift Costs Concentrated in One Year. One of the two major results of the study was a descriptive comparison of the allocation categories (market-technique-gift type) regarding their detailed solicitation processes. The analysis of those categories where the solicitation process extended beyond one year revealed an interesting relationship between costs and benefits. Although fund-raising activity costs might have covered a three- to five-year period, and the gifts might have come in over another three- to five-year period, a great majority of the costs were associated with a particular year. The pattern shown in Table 9.1 consistently appeared. The pattern shows that the costs involved in a

Table 9.1. Northwestern University Typical
Long-Term Solicitation Pattern.
(In dollars)

	Year 1	Year 2	Year 3	Year 4	Year 5	Year 6
Costs	100	200	2,000	200	100	100
Gifts			10,000	20,000	10,000	5,000

solicitation stream are concentrated in one year, usually the same year as the pledge commitment. The pledges are paid off over a multiyear period. This concentration of development resources in one year justified the calculation of the present value of the pledge commitment based on the year of highest development activity. Without a fixed point for the costs, an accurate determination of the present value of the pledge would be difficult.

In addition, I found that many gifts were associated with no or very little activity cost during the six-year period examined by the study. These gifts may have been associated with costs incurred by areas outside of the development office (president's office, dean's office, faculty, and so forth), or outside of the study's date range. Low-development-cost gifts accounted for approximately one-third of the total gift dollars from all markets; however, most of the low-development-cost gifts that did exist were concentrated in the other-nonindividual market.

This result may seem to cause a problem in making the fund-raising management process work; however, the strategic planning method takes this potential problem into account. For example, at Northwestern, the other-nonindividual market was eliminated from the analysis because no development officer spends time with this market, and it did not make sense to consider allocating resources to this category. The other cases were handled by estimating the level of low-development-cost gifts for each category and using that as a base level for the model.

Optimal Solution Shifted Resources to Long-Term Programs. The second major finding was that the optimal solution of the final model shifted resources toward the long-term fund-raising programs, represented by categories that dealt with major gifts from corporations, foundations, and alumni, along with irrevocable gifts from individual alumni and nonalumni. Therefore, the solution also shifted resources away from the programs for phone-a-thons, direct mail, personal solicitation for annual gifts, and personal solicitation for major outright gifts from nonalumni.

The First Consideration: Delay Factors. Analysis of the delay factors in the solicitation process revealed great differences among the various categories in the study. Most categories had delays within the study's six-year time frame. However, some categories had delays that appeared to go beyond six years. For example, direct-mail and phone-a-thon responses showed less than a year's delay between the asking and the gift. But major gifts from all sources had delays of four and five years from major solicitation activity until the final payment on a multiyear pledge. Moreover, bequests and irrevocable trusts could not be analyzed properly within the six-year period. A minimum of fifteen years of data is probably required to determine the usual delay factors for these categories.

Study results support the idea that development is a very long-term process and that, in some instances, the longer the delay, the greater the payout. Nevertheless, at certain levels of capital cost, the investment may not prove effective. For example, actively soliciting bequests where the payout has been shown to occur twenty-five years later may not be cost effective when considering the cost of capital (8–10 percent most recently) to support the activity and the revocable nature of a bequest commitment. The methodology in this study provides a start for determining the efficiencies of the trade-offs that occur when accepting various delay periods.

The Second Consideration: Priority Levels. The results showed some differentiation between categories regarding priority levels. For example, major gifts personally solicited from alumni was the category with the highest priority level, bringing in gifts with values well beyond their simple cash value. The four types of added value discussed earlier were ranked as follows: (1) priority designation of the gift, (2) long-term nature of the transaction, (3) related contacts, and (4) public relations. The freeform area of the survey further supported this result, which indicated that the designation of a gift is the most important added value.

The gift designation that was overwhelmingly the top priority for Northwestern was unrestricted operating funds. However, this is probably the least popular designation for any prospective major gift donor, creating a very difficult situation. By creating a separate multiplier to give extra value to unrestricted gifts, the study tested the model's sensitivity to changes in this value. The results showed very little change in optimal resource allocation strategy when moving from a low level of added value ($1.10 per $1.00) to a very high level of added value ($1.50 per $1.00).

The potential for future gifts was the second most important added value. Although this added value was not considered independently, as was the designation value, when it was incorporated into the weighted overall added-value multiplier, the same results occurred. There was very little change in optimal resource allocation strategy when moving from a low level to a high level of overall added value (including the potential for future gifts). In addition, short-term programs were still less cost effective as compared to most long-term programs.

The Third Consideration: Crossover Effects. Besides the very strong relationship found between corporate matching gifts and the direct-mail and phone-a-thon categories, very few crossover effects were found. At a very low level, nonalumni and parent individuals were used as a part of soliciting corporate gifts. In this way, resources allocated to working with an alumni volunteer solicitor would not result in gifts recorded in an alumni category. Instead, the gifts would be found in a corporate category. Since only the crossover effects among markets were examined, crossover effects among techniques or gift types have yet to be determined. Questions that must be studied more carefully in order to clearly understand various crossover relationships over a multiyear time frame include: What effect do ten years of phone-a-thon calls have on personal major gift fundraising efforts? What was the effect if they were successful calls? What was the effect if the prospect became irritated after having to say no to a volunteer three years in a row?

Past Fund-Raising Research

The derived functional forms for each category, which represented the answer to the study's main question—What is the relationship between costs and benefits in a development operation?—generally agreed with the results of past fund-raising research. The general form of the relationship as described by Paton (1986); the correlation between fund-raising expenditures and gift income as found by Leslie (1969), Pickett (1977), Leslie and Ramey (1985), and Loessin (1987); the cost effectiveness of the direct-mail process as shown by Soukup (1983); the need to give priority resources to large gifts as concluded by McCaskey and Dunn (1983); and the demonstration of a net benefit in a deferred-gift program by Fink (1982) were all substantiated in the Northwestern study.

    One area in which the results did differ was the regression analysis of the solicitation process time delay. While Massy and Frank (Kotler, 1971, p. 127) found that the most recent periods of effort correlated most with the current sales response level, the results in the Northwestern study show that for long-term gift transactions—for example, major and irrevocable gifts—the periods of highest correlation may be removed several years from the period of gift response.

Policy Implications and Future Research

Before the Northwestern study, fund-raising research focused on the effectiveness of a particular market, program, or technique. Deferred giving, phone-a-thons, and direct mail were all studied as separate entities, with connections that were only inferred through the development staff's anecdotal experiences. The results of this study suggest that future research projects need to consider how a particular program relates to the entire fund-raising effort at a nonprofit before those projects make conclusions about that program's cost effectiveness.

It is not enough to say that a particular program costs $.25 per $1.00 raised. The question that must be answered is whether the marginal cost-gift relationship is reasonable compared to all other programs at the institution. Having ten fund-raising programs that are *individually* cost effective is no longer enough. Rather, the program balance that will achieve optimal gift levels should be investigated in any study of a fund-raising operation's cost effectiveness.

Studies into fund raising should concentrate on those factors that can be modified relatively easily by the institution and that have the potential to increase the dollars raised. Also, because the total dollars allocated to development are typically relatively fixed or only slowly rising, it is important to consider the best allocation of current resources as well as the addition of new resources. Obviously, expanding a nonprofit's research data base to include fifteen to twenty years of information from within that nonprofit—and then from several institutions—and using that information for further analysis of the solicitation process as modeled in this study would be an appropriate direction.

Certainly, much remains to be done in terms of addressing methodological problems encountered in this study. For example, one area that needs further investigation is the determination of the overall value of nondollar benefits of gifts in the areas of public relations, long-term relationships, secondary contacts, and priority. In the Northwestern University study, a range from $1.00 to $1.50 on the dollar was used as a multiplier. A more accurate value is needed. Besides this particular aspect, the whole area of added value requires more research.

Fund-Raising Strategy Implications

This study implies that it is no longer possible to use casual analysis of past experience to determine the most cost-effective way to organize a nonprofit institution's fund-raising effort. This ad hoc approach to resource allocation is inherently biased by the psychological influence of such factors as the immediate income and response offered by short-term fund raising and the enthusiasm that surrounds large gift transactions. The typical reporting structure of a fund-raising campaign, where a cash-in mentality prevails and low-development-cost gifts are mixed with those that involved considerable development cost, is also a source of bias. The fact that a particular program is cost effective within its own boundaries does not imply that it should be funded. For optimal results, the balance between high-potential high-cost long-term programs and low-potential low-cost short-term programs needs to be determined analytically.

Although I cannot conclude from this study that all nonprofit organizations should move toward a more long-term strategy, I do suggest that any fund-raising program should:

• Bring in analytical tools such as the techniques developed in this study to provide the basis for a strategic planning process.
• Adjust its reporting process to show development progress rather than cash-in numbers.
• Depending on the results of the analysis, be prepared to change its personnel policies from a short-term to a long-term strategy.

Bring In Analytical Tools. In order to be able to study the costs and benefits in the solicitation process at a nonprofit, it is clear that a radical change in data collection policy should be initiated. However, the costs of a massive retrospective collection process, going back several years in time, may be too great to justify the analysis. Therefore, what is needed is a simple way to record solicitation and cultivation costs across the entire prospect population *as they occur.* A similar process already exists for recording income using a gift-processing operation. Unless contact costs are recorded at the activity transaction level, accurate response functions will be very difficult to determine.

Cost transactions need to be recorded over many years to allow patterns in the solicitation process to become apparent.

For example, the length of the nonzero solicitation streams for major-gift fund-raising approaches three or four years, and for certain gifts — such as bequests — I assume lengths in excess of ten to fifteen years would not be uncommon. This means that the planning process should be set up for the long haul and not assumed to be necessary for only a few years. Only when sufficient variations in the resources allocated over time have been recorded can patterns of receiving the corresponding gifts be determined.

The cost-transaction records probably should not be a sampled set, but rather should be recorded for the entire population. As development professionals realize, the giving of a major gift does not occur very often in the population; it is a rare event situation. Lindahl and Winship (1991) found that there were only sixty-one donors, out of a population of 140,000 alumni, who gave over $100,000 to Northwestern University in a three-year period. In my study at Northwestern, I tried to take this fact into account by systematically selecting my sample so that two subpopulations (top prospects and bottom prospects) were considered separately. Even so, the number of cases in a sample set would have to be so great that it would probably be more cost effective in the long run to set up the system at the beginning so that it can handle the whole population. The benefits that will arise from using the data for other purposes, such as solicitation tracking, further support maintaining full cost records on the whole population.

Solicitation activity cost records can be used at all levels of cost accountability — from the market level, to the program level, down to the development officer level. At the individual officer level, the data could be organized to provide a month-by-month accounting of visits, proposals, letters, and phone calls and to show donor responsiveness in terms of pledge commitments, gifts, and bequest expectancies. This information will provide a much more accurate and fair method of determining merit salary increases and will help in developing better fund-raising techniques. Currently, only the total results in a program, area, or market are usually available for merit evaluation and program-development judgments. If there are a large number of nonsolicited gifts (or gifts solicited outside of the formal development operation), these total gift figures can be extremely misleading.

The process of collecting cost information should follow these guidelines:

- Ensure that every development officer participates by providing basic information for each contact.
- Record activities in the main data base so they can easily be compared to corresponding gift information.
- Eliminate redundant manual reporting schemes and have everyone (including management) use the output generated from the main files.
- Provide data entry support at a level that turns around record entry on a daily basis.
- Ensure that on-line screens, analysis reports, and an ad hoc inquiry system are all available before officers are asked to begin sending in contact records.
- Standardize activity costs, but yet allow for variations.
- Automate the process of recording direct-mail and phone-a-thon cost transactions, so that a record will be generated every time a label or phone-a-thon information sheet is produced.
- Keep the process simple.

Implementing such a cost-accounting system over a five-to-ten-year period will provide an excellent base of information to use in analyzing resource allocations. The methodology used in this study could be applied to the new data base, creating more accurate response functions for each category. Further, since the costs will be recorded at the transaction level, other groupings of categories — such as school, area, or regional office — could easily be analyzed.

Adjust the Reporting Process. The reporting structure in non-profits should change as well. Reliance on cash-in figures to report development progress should be supplemented by an adjusted development progress report. Each category of transaction should be modified to provide a current-year equivalent value: pledges should be reduced to the current value of the stream of pledge payments, pledge payments themselves eliminated from the report, irrevocable-trust gifts adjusted to reflect their current value, bequest expectancies reduced based on expected year of receipt, bequest received dollars removed from the report, and outright gifts counted at full value.

The report should also strip away gifts that were not generated directly by development resources. One of the most important results of this study was the determination of the amount of low-development-cost gifts occurring at Northwestern University during the six years examined by the study. As part of determining the formulas for each category, the gift dollars that were associated with little or no direct solicitation were isolated. Approximately one-third of the reported gift totals were in this group.

If this result holds for nonprofits generally, then the ramifications for fund-raising operation assessment are considerable. For example, in higher education, when the total gift figures in the year-end Council for Aid to Education (CFAE) report are used for stating how well an institution's development operation is doing, the possible error in this number is potentially very large. Suppose an institution raised $60 million, including $20 million of low-development-cost gifts, in 1986, and $50 million, including $5 million of low-development-cost gifts, in 1987. If the low-development-cost transactions are not reported separately (and currently they are not separately reported), the obvious conclusion would be that the performance of this institution's development office had dropped precipitously. But in reality, the performance of the office is up—by somewhere over 12 percent. Combine this difficulty with the problems that surround the delay factors and with the different ways certain schools report corporate and foundation contracts as gifts, and it becomes almost impossible to use CFAE type numbers (as currently calculated) to assess performance or, especially, to compare performance from one institution to another. However, most of the research being done across institutional boundaries uses this type of number in its analyses — a disconcerting thought indeed.

The solution to the problem is available but not easily implemented. To remove low-development-cost gifts from a gift total requires a closer tracking of the relationship between solicitation costs and gift dollars. A cost-accounting program that systematically records all solicitation and cultivation contacts and their related costs for the entire prospect pool would be difficult to implement across all nonprofits. The definition of the level of costs that would constitute a low-development cost would also be problematic. Perhaps the only reasonable short-term solution would be a warning placed at the beginning of any cross-institutional report on fund-raising progress: "These numbers do not accurately reflect the performance of the corresponding development operations at the following institutions. Do not use them for research into comparative fund-raising effectiveness."

Personnel Policies Change. Where a more long-term strategy is indicated, the specific strategy recommended for nonprofits will usually require changes in personnel policy. Recruitment practices should be modified to hire for the long run, not for the quick fix. Development operations should hire people who can relate to the 1 to 10 percent of the prospect pool who are major gift prospects. They should hire people who enjoy involving alumni or patrons in the life of the institution and have the patience and persistence to work for large gifts from individuals, corporations, and foundations. In today's job market, this hiring policy can not always be implemented. The supply of professional fund raisers is low compared to the high demand. Even so, the goal of hiring for the long term should be upheld as the ideal.

In addition, using short-term or cash-in results as the main evaluation criteria can cause an excellent staff member to look ineffective or an average staff member to look outstanding. Personnel should be evaluated both on long-term (two- or three-year) results and on how well and how often they relate to the prospects.

Conclusions for Universities

Universities are distinguished from other nonprofit organizations in several ways, some of which are central to the issue of effectively increasing gifts to the institution. An alumni body provides a unique prospect market. The emotional ties that are formed during a person's years of changing from a child to an adult, the eventual network of alumni business contacts, and the fifty-to-sixty-year time span over which fund raising can occur all serve to make the higher education setting a unique place for fund raising. Furthermore, the extensive research being done year in and year out at a university in many areas of study provides a unique potential for the development of key long-term funding relationships with corporations and foundations.

However, anyone spending much time in university development becomes well aware that universities tend to handle fund raising by looking to short-term results. They tend to allocate development resources myopically, constantly driven by the need to enhance the current year's operating budget. This year's goals, this year's results, this year's cash-in become the driving forces in the resource allocation process, rather than some realistic measure of actual benefits.

Shift Toward Long-Term Programs. The results of this study show that even for universities like Northwestern with a strong history of major-gift fund raising, there is a need for a dramatic shift away from short-term programs such as direct mail and phone-a-thons, and toward long-term programs such as major gifts from alumni, corporations, and foundations and toward irrevocable-trust gifts. The fact that the study took into account the delay factors involved in major-gift and irrevocable-trust fund raising, the added value of the unrestricted dollars that result from short-term programs, and the crossover effect of the annual fund on corporate gifts due to corporate matching-gift programs further highlights the dramatic nature of the study results.

By allocating their resources differently, universities can take advantage of the unique long-term relationships that are associated with the alumni, foundation, and corporate markets.

With tnis change in strategy will come the potential for greatly increased gift dollars to flow to higher education institutions throughout the United States.

Fund-raising expert Gary Evans supports this positive conclusion as well in these words of advice to university presidents: "Because major gifts will probably produce 80 percent or more of your gift results, you should make certain that the budget for the development office has a significant portion allocated for donor research, cultivation, and involvement of major gift prospects. And the budget should not be disproportionate in its support of annual giving programs, even though they may generate more immediate results" (Fisher and Quehl, 1989, p. 141).

Obviously there is risk associated with a long-term fund-raising strategy. By investing current dollars into fund raising that may take three to twenty years to pay out, the university risks its short-term financial security. Also, the external and internal conditions faced by a university can change dramatically from year to year. However, the results of this study suggest that simply reallocating resources will provide net increases in the millions of dollars. Even if these figures are high by as much as 50 percent, the potential gain appears to be well worth the potential risks. Most large institutions with sizeable endowments can certainly handle a dip in the annual-fund revenues over an approximately two- to five-year period while the investment in the enhanced long-term program comes to fruition.

Break Down the Pyramid. The potential loss of the base of the traditional fund-raising pyramid if the short-term annual-fund programs are reduced is also seen as a major risk. The traditional wisdom among development officers is that alumni donors are guided through a lifelong process that starts with an annual-fund gift solicited via direct mail or phone-a-thon and develops by way of gift-club levels and reunion gifts to, eventually, a major gift or estate gift. Although there are currently no formal published studies that support or reject this pattern, traditional wisdom assumes these connections exist.

If the pattern is accurate, one of the potential problems associated with a reduced base is the lack of capable major-gift prospects in the future. But if the annual-fund program is reduced wisely, the reduction would mainly represent the hardcore never givers and those who are still at the base of the pyramid, giving very low-level gifts, even after several decades of contact. This group has not responded as development officers would have hoped to mailings and phone calls over the first ten to twenty years after graduation. In contrast, the effect of the reduction on the steadily developing core of strong high-level annual givers would be nil. They have established excellent giving patterns and will continue to be asked even in a reduced annual-fund program. Moreover, they invariably will form the true base of the pyramid and, one hopes, the apex as well. In the final analysis, less than 10 percent of the population will be needed in the long run to provide the major-gift prospect base.

The argument could still be made that limiting the size of the annual-fund solicitation effort will diminish the filtering effect of annual requests. By casting a wide net over many years, the university ensures that major gift prospects self-identify themselves. But other ways exist to identify these donors. Peer review programs, such as those at Stanford and Northwestern, where influential alumni are asked to rate their classmates as to gift potential have been shown to do an excellent job of filtering. Estate-planning mailings that describe the various giving plans can be regularly sent out to alumni and can include a reply card for self-identification. By allowing donors to self-identify themselves, these programs target the population most likely to make a major deferred or estate gift — not just a larger annual gift. Research on donors of these gifts (Lindahl, 1991) shows that past outright giving is not a significant predictor of planned giving, hence these techniques of identifying planned-giving prospects are particularly useful, and they would not be negatively affected by a reduction in the short-term fund-raising programs.

Certainly no study should suggest that annual-fund fund raising be ignored completely. A balanced approach is essential. David R. Dunlop states this clearly in his discussion of what he calls the "ultimate gift": "The habits of giving, and the sense of commitment encouraged by regular [annual] and special gift-giving help set the stage for securing ultimate gifts. This requires a balanced development program, one that includes speculative and individualized fund raising as well as nurturing fund raising" (Fisher and Quehl, 1989, p. 178). However, my study does suggest that there may be diminishing returns from those who give the lower level gifts. For mature fund-raising programs such as Northwestern's, the resources allocated to the annual fund could be reduced without serious harm to the pyramid either in actual donors or in the filtering effect.

Summing Up

The Northwestern study provides results that are helpful to nonprofits when they are considering general fund-raising strategies. The strategic planning methodology developed through the study allows development officers to take advantage of the techniques used in the analogous sales force allocation problem. Fund-raising practitioners can use their intuition and experience in an organized rigorous fashion, rather than in an ad hoc or anecdotal way, when their organizations make use of this methodology. Moving the strategic planning process into the heart of the fund-raising operation will help to support the mission of nonprofits around the globe, and through them, will help to make the world a better place for all of us.

References

AAFRC Trust for Philanthropy. *Giving USA*. New York: AAFRC Trust for Philanthropy, 1991.

Bryson, J. *Strategic Planning for Public and Nonprofit Organizations: A Guide to Strengthening and Sustaining Organizational Achievement.* San Francisco: Jossey-Bass, 1988.

Carbone, R. F. *Fund Raisers of Academe.* College Park: University of Maryland Clearinghouse for Research on Fund Raising, 1987.

Fink, N. S., and Metzler, H. C. *The Costs and Benefits of Deferred Giving.* New York: Columbia University Press, 1982.

Fisher, J. L., and Quehl, G. H. *The President and Fund Raising.* New York: Macmillan, 1989.

Galloway, T. D. "Comment on 'Comparison of Current Planning Theories: Counterparts and Contradictions' by B. M. Hudson." *Journal of the American Planning Association,* 1979, *45*(4), 399–402.

Herman, R., Weaver, E., and Heimovics, R. "Judgments of Nonprofit Organization Effectiveness." *1991 Annual ARNOVA Conference Proceedings — Collaboration: The Vital Link Across Practice, Research and the Disciplines.* Pullman, Wash.: ARNOVA, 1991.

Howe, F. *The Board Member's Guide to Fund Raising: What Every Trustee Needs to Know About Raising Money.* San Francisco: Jossey-Bass, 1991.

Kotler, P. *Marketing Decision Making: A Model Building Approach.* New York: Holt, Rinehart & Winston, 1971.

Leslie, J. W. *Focus on Understanding and Support: A Study in College Management.* Washington, D.C.: American College Public Relations Association, 1969.

Leslie, L. L., and Ramey, G. "When Donors Give: How Giving Changes in Good and Bad Times." *CASE Currents,* 1985, *11*(9), 25–26.

Lev, M. "Stanford Gets U. of C. Provost." *Chicago Tribune,* Mar. 19, 1992, sec. 2, p. 11.

Lindahl, W. E. *Resource Allocation in University Fund Raising.* Doctoral Dissertation, Northwestern University, Evanston, Ill.: University Microfilms International, 1990.

Lindahl, W. E. "Differentiating Planned and Major Gift Prospects." In *Connections.* Washington, D.C.: American Association of Prospect Research, 1991.

Lindahl, W. E., and Winship, C. "Predictive Models for Annual Fund and Major Gift Fund Raising." Paper presented at the Association for Research on Nonprofit Organizations and Voluntary Action (ARNOVA) conference, Chicago, 1991.

Loessin, B. A., and others. "Identifying Peer Institutions for Comparative Evaluation of Fund Raising Effectiveness." Paper presented at the AIR Forum, Kansas City, Mo., 1987.

Lorange, P. *Corporate Planning: An Executive Viewpoint.* Englewood Cliffs, N.J.: Prentice Hall, 1980.

McCaskey, C., and Dunn, J. A., Jr. "Look into My Crystal Cathode Ray Tube: Computer Models Make Annual Giving Predictions Easy." *CASE Currents,* 1983, *9*(3), 38–42.

Murray, D. J. *The Guaranteed Fund-Raising System.* Boston: American Institute of Management, 1987.

Paton, G. J. "Microeconomic Perspectives Applied to Developmental Planning and Management." *New Directions for Institutional Research,* 1986, (51), 17–38.

Pickett, W. L. "An Assessment of the Effectiveness of Fund Raising Policies of Private Undergraduate Colleges." Doctoral dissertation, University of Denver, 1977.

Soukup, D. J. "A Markov Analysis of Fund-Raising Alternatives." *Journal of Marketing Research,* 1983, *20,* 314–319.

Sinha, P., and Zoltners, A. *Addressing the Issues of Sales Force Size and Structure.* Evanston, Ill.: ZS Associates, 1986.

Steinberg, R. "Optimal Fundraising by Nonprofit Firms." *1985 Spring Research Forum Working Papers Conference Volume.* New York: INDEPENDENT SECTOR and the United Way Institute, 1985.

Steinberg, R. "Economic Perspectives on Regulation of Charitable Solicitations." *Case Western Reserve Law Review, 39,* 1988–89.

Stuart, D. G. "Rational Urban Planning: Problems and Prospects." *Urban Affairs Quarterly,* Dec. 1969, *5,* 151–182.

Taylor, K. (ed.). *CASE Currents,* 1991, *17*(8), 15–62.

Tidwell, G. "Fund Raising Ethics." *Atlanta Journal,* Apr. 14, 1991, p. A3.

Zoltners, A., and Sinha, P. "Integer Programming Models for Sales Resource Allocation." *Management Science,* 1980, *26,* 242–260.

Index